BLACK RELIGIOUS EXPERIENCE

CONVERSATIONS ON DOUBLE CONSCIOUSNESS AND THE WORK OF GRANT SHOCKLEY

CHARLES R. FOSTER
AND FRED SMITH
WITH
GRANT S. SHOCKLEY

Abingdon Press
Nashville

BLACK RELIGIOUS EXPERIENCE
CONVERSATIONS ON DOUBLE CONSCIOUSNESS AND THE WORK
OF GRANT SHOCKLEY

This book is printed on elemental-chlorine–free paper.

Library of Congress Cataloging-in-Publication Data

Foster, Charles R., 1937-
  Black Religious Experience :Conversations on double consciousness and the work of Grant Shockley / Charles R. Foster and Fred Smith; with Grant S. Shockley.
     p. cm.
Includes bibliographical references.
ISBN 0-687-04479-0 (alk. paper)
  1. African American churches. 2. Christian education. I. Smith, Fred, 1951- II. Shockley, Grant S., 1919- III. Title.

  BR563.N4 F66 2003
  268'.089'96073—dc21

                                                                    2003011050

All scripture quotations unless noted otherwise are taken from the *New Revised Standard Version of the Bible*, copyright 1989, by the Division of Christian Education of the National Council of the Churches of Christ in the United States of America. Used by permission. All rights reserved.

Scripture quotations noted KJV are from the King James or Authorized Version of the Bible.

The essay on pages 29-32 was originally published as "The Black Experience and Black Religion" in *The Black Church* 2(1974), pp. 94-97.

The esay on pages 32-43 was originally published as "Christian Education and the Black Church" in *The Journal of the Interdenominational Theological Center* 2 (1974), pp. 75-85. Copyright © by The Journal of the Interdenominational Theological Center. Used by permission.

The essay on pages 48-61 was originally published as "Transcendence and Mystery in the Third World," in Earl D. C. Brewer, ed., *Transcendence and Mystery* (New York: IDOC/America, Inc., 1973), pp. 76-88.

The essay on pages 61-64 was originally published as "Liberation Theology, Black Theology, and Religious Education," in Martin J. Taylor, ed., *Foundations for Christian Education in an Era of Change* (Nashville: Abingdon Press, 1976), pp. 80-95.

The essay on pages 64-66 was originally a lecture published as "Christian Education and the Black Church," in Charles R. Foster, Ethel R. Johnson, and Grant S. Shockley, *Christian Education Journey of Black Americans: Past, Present, Future* (Nashville: Discipleship Resources, 1985), pp. 1-2.

The essay on pages 66-73 was originally a lecture published as "Black Theology and Religious Education," Randolph Crump Miller, ed., *Theologies of Religious Education* (Birmingham: Religious Education Press, 1995), pp. 314-21.

The essay on pages 79-82 was originally a lecture published as "Christian Education and the Black Church," Charles R. Foster, Ethel R. Johnson, and Grant S. Shockley, *Christian Education Journey of Black Americans: Past, Present, Future* (Nashville: Discipleship Resources, 1985), pp. 14-17.

The essay on pages 82-86 was originally a lecture published as "From Emancipation to Transformation to Consummation: A Black Perspective," in Marlene Mayr, ed., *Does the Church Really Want Religious Education?* (Birmingham: Religious Education Press, 1988), pp. 242-46.

The essay on pages 86-97 was originally a lecture published as "Challenge from Multiculturalism," in Charles R. Foster, ed., *Ethnicity in the Education of the Church* (Nashville: Scarritt Press, 1987), pp. 29-39.

The essay on pages 97-106 was originally published as "Religious Pluralism and Religious Education: A Black Protestant Perspective," in Norma H. Thomapson, ed., *Religious Pluralism and Religious Education* (Birmingham: Religious Education Press, 1988), pp. 152-61

The essay on pages 106-11 was originally published as "Black Pastoral Leadership in Religious Education," in Robert L. Browning, ed., *The Pastor as Religious Educator* (Birmingham: Religious Education Press, 1989), pp. 201-6.

The essay on pages 111-23 was originally published as "Black Theology and Religious Education," in Randolph Crump Miller, ed., *Theology of Religious Education* (Birmingham: Religious Education Press, 1995), pp. 321-22 and 324-35.

03 04 05 06 07 08 09 10 11 12—10 9 8 7 6 5 4 3 2 1

MANUFACTURED IN THE UNITED STATES OF AMERICA

CONTENTS

Acknowledgments 7

Foreword 9

Introduction
   Remembering the Life and Work of Grant S. Shockley 15

Section I: A Way of Thinking About the
      Black Religious Education Experience 25
   Introduction 25
   Double Consciousness 29
   Contextuality 32

Section II: Sources for a Liberative Religious Education 45
   Introduction 45
   Transcendence and Mystery in the Third World 48
   Liberation Theology, Black Theology, and
      Religious Education 61
   Christian Education and the Black Church 64
   Black Theology and Religious Education 66

Section III: The Quest for a Model 75
   Introduction 75
   The Confluence of Black and Liberation Theologies
      and Liberative Pedagogies 79

Assumptions 82
Challenge from Multiculturalism 86
The Challenge of Religious Pluralism 97
Primary Characteristics 106
A Basic Framework 111

**Section IV: To Create the Beloved Community: A Prophetic
Christian Education for the Twenty-first Century . . 125**

Appendix
Grant S. Shockley's Curriculum Vita 153

Notes 157

Selected Bibliography 169

ACKNOWLEDGMENTS

Several people have had an important role in this project. Doris Shockley, wife of Grant Shockley, encouraged us to take on the project and gave us access to his papers and files. We discovered, consequently, that throughout his professional life he had been a consummate collector of articles, books, and other resources on the black religious experience. Two of Shockley's closest friends through most of his career, Bishop James S. Thomas and Ethel R. Johnson, illumined the story of his life and provided many clues to the interpretation of his work. Students in our classes helped us probe themes in his writing. Anne Streaty Wimberly and other religious education scholars have provided persistent encouragement.

It did not take long before we became aware of the special role that James Michael Lee, editor and publisher of the Religious Education Press, played in making Shockley's writings available to the larger religious education public. Several extended quotations of Shockley's writings reproduced in this book come from essays he wrote for Religious Education Press at Lee's invitation. Through Religious Education Press, Lee encouraged Shockley's most mature writing at a time when black religious educators had difficulty finding publishers for their work. We are similarly appreciative for the support and editorial oversight of the staff of Abingdon Press. They have made our dream for this publication a reality.

FOREWORD

In 1903 W. E. B. DuBois wrote *The Souls of Black Folk*. In that work he developed a lens through which descendants of the African slave trade in North America could make sense of their experience with the patterns of domination in the cultural heritage of those who had migrated to the new continent from Europe. That perspective on their experience he called "double consciousness."

> The Negro is a sort of seventh son, born with a veil, and gifted with second-sight in this American world—a world which yields him no true self-consciousness, but only lets him see himself through the revelation of the other world. It is a peculiar sensation, this double-consciousness, this sense of always looking at one's self through the eyes of others, of measuring one's soul by the tape of a world that looks on in amused contempt and pity. One ever feels his twoness—an American, a Negro; two souls, two thoughts, two unreconciled strivings; two warring ideals in one dark body, whose dogged strength alone keeps it from being torn asunder.[1]

DuBois's insight was powerful. It has influenced the thinking of contemporary scholars seeking to understand something of the dynamics of dominance and oppression not only in the relationship of white and black folk in the United States but in any exercise of power of one group over another. It also provides a framework for this work on the religious education experience of Black U.S. American Protestants. In the pages that follow we seek to tell the story of Grant Shockley's quest for a model of Christian education rooted in and responsive to the religious experience of African Americans. Although this story is relatively unknown—even in black congregations—it is an important one. Shockley was the primary interpreter of religious education in the black church to the larger academic and church worlds in the second half of the twentieth century.[2] His approach was both theological and historical. He sought to discern what we would now call the Africentric origins of the church's education. In this effort, his quest illumines something of the struggle black scholars in religion faced in bringing to voice the distinctive contribution of African Americans to the larger discussions of religious life in the nation.

Throughout his career Shockley was all too conscious that as a descendent of the African diaspora in the United States, his efforts to retrieve the heritage of the black Christian religious education experience occurred within the framework of a predominantly white, Anglo-European religious and cultural environment. His context reinforced this awareness. He was black encountering the privileges and power of those who were white. He was ordained to the ministry of a predominantly white denomination with a significant and segregated black constituency. Much of his career was spent in leadership roles in predominantly white ecclesial and academic institutions. The primary audience for his writing included professional and academic religious educators of European heritage employed in dominant culture institutions.

During his lifetime Shockley never fully realized his dream of a model of Christian education originating in the religious experience of Black Americans. And yet, in the trajectory of his work, we can discern the workings of a first rate mind struggling against the oppressive domination of double consciousness on his imagination. It is in the unfolding of the course of his thinking that we encounter both the significance of his work for the education in contemporary black congregations and a larger understanding of the religious education of all Christians. A closer look at his work reveals a scholar who begins his quest for the historical roots of education in the black religious experience in the structures and practices of religious education in dominant culture churches. He strives hard against that framework, however, and over the years, gradually moves toward an increasingly Africentric orientation to his understanding of that educational experience. In that effort he was not entirely alone. James D. Tyms at Howard University Divinity School; Paul Nichols at Virginia Union Theological Seminary; Olivia Pearl Stokes, the first black staff member of the National Council of Churches; Mary Love with the AME Zion Church; and Yvonne Delk of the United Church of Christ were prominent colleagues sharing Shockley's passion for understanding the heritage of black church education and his quest for black church models of religious education. Through Shockley's writings, however, we have the most comprehensive picture of this journey among these black religious educators. For this reason, we intend to trace the trajectory of his thought in religious education and to project a proposal for a view of religious education emerging from the heritage and experience of the black church.

The story we have to tell is larger than the story of an unfolding view of religious education. The Africentric perspective that increasingly influenced Shockley's work functions paradigmatically for many African American religious leaders. It is the story of a scholarly journey through double consciousness as personal and shared burden to double consciousness as gift to church and academic communities. In the telling of this story we rely on Shockley's writings to illumine the development of his thought. We do this, in part, to make his words accessible to readers.

At the same time Grant Shockley's life and work provides the catalyst to a second story—one that we must also tell. This second story reveals something of his teaching style. In the classroom or in his office he would typically be engaged in conversation with students or colleagues. They would be exploring together some insight into the heritage of education in the black church, some theological or cultural issue, or some question about the dynamics of racism in cross-cultural religious education. When someone said something he considered insightful, he would lean forward and say, "Why don't you find out more about that?" He encouraged his students to do the research, write a paper, or report their findings to the rest of the class. He would then lead his students into a deeper engagement with the insight or question.

This book has its origins in those conversations. Indeed we have organized it as a conversation—a conversation with Grant Shockley at the center. We are engaged in this conversation as two Christian religious educators—one black and one white—whose encounter with each other illumines the influence of double-consciousness on the ways we think about religious education in a racially and culturally diverse society. Through our conversation we seek to make evident the development of Shockley's thinking about education in and through the church as he negotiated his way through the double consciousness he brought to this task. It is as black and white that we approach this task to reflect the context in which Shockley worked out his own understanding of the purposes and mission of Christian religious education and to illumine the sources and influence of his thought. We bring to our conversations with Shockley's writings the mutuality of our engagement with our own embeddedness in the patterns of double consciousness found in the responses of American U.S. minority and majority peoples to each other.

The format of the book within this framework is straightforward. We begin with a conversation with Bishop James S. Thomas and Ethel R. Johnson. They shared a friendship of more than fifty years with Shockley. Thomas, a retired bishop of the United Methodist Church, was a schoolmate of Shockley's at the Drew Theological Seminary. Johnson first met Shockley at the church in Harlem where he was serving as an assistant pastor. She later joined him on the staff of the Janes Methodist Church in Brooklyn.

These two longtime friends and colleagues illumine something of the story of his life. The rest of the book centers on the unfolding story of Shockley's thinking about religious education in the black church and community. It is divided into four sections. The first section explores the method or perspective that informed his work. The second illumines the sources that informed his thinking. The third explicates the model or strategy emerging from his work over the course of his career. In each of these three sections we seek to establish through a conversation with each other the context for the selections of Shockley's writing we have chosen to engage the theme of the section. We could not, of course, include everything he wrote. Instead we have chosen segments from a number of essays that illumine the trajectory of his thinking about religious education over a twenty-five-year period. The reader will encounter some thematic repetition in Shockley's writing. It is even more evident in the full text of his essays. It reflects his recognition that, with every essay, he had to introduce a new audience to the black religious experience, while developing at the same time, a new way of thinking about Christian education in the black church.

We have included a fourth section. Shockley had hoped to write a book on the black religious education experience after his retirement. In retirement he taught several classes at the Candler School of Theology that began to define the shape and content of that book. He did not realize this dream, however, before his death. In this final section we have therefore taken up the task of projecting the trajectory of his thinking into the future. Although we take full responsibility for this chapter, we also believe it is faithful to the growing edges of his work.

One further note: in the editorial process we recast all the endnotes so that they follow a common format. We have left intact however, the editorial practices regarding designations of gender and the use of Afrocentric/Africentric and black/Black in each selection at the time of its publication. In this decision the collection of his essays makes evident the evolution of a new vocabulary for the black religious education experience in the United States.

Fred Smith and Charles R. Foster

INTRODUCTION

Remembering the Life and Work of Grant S. Shockley:
An Interview with Bishop James S. Thomas and Ethel R. Johnson

Foster: Grant and I first met in a gathering of United Methodist professors of Christian education in the 1970s. Our friendship grew, however, during our collaboration in planning two conferences that led to the publication of *Ethnicity in the Education of the Church* (Scarritt Press, 1987) and *Working with Black Youth* (Abingdon, 1989). When I heard that he was returning to Atlanta to live after his retirement from Duke Divinity School, I asked him to teach two courses a year in the Christian education program at Candler School of Theology. In that setting I hoped he would have the opportunity to use the classroom to test his thinking about Christian education in the black church for a major publication in the field. In our collaboration we had a distinctive working relationship. He was always the mentor, both seeing possibilities for shaping the future of the field and suggesting readings to deepen my thinking and projects to focus my energy. This book is the natural outcome of that relationship. Since he died before the book was written, I have wanted to make sure that his legacy is not lost.

Smith: My own relationship to Grant was more as a student than a colleague. I first met him while he was the president of Philander Smith College in Arkansas. I was a student from the Perkins School of Theology doing my intern year at Pulaski Heights United Methodist

Church in Little Rock. He wanted me to come to the college to be chaplain—an invitation I did not accept. Much later, here in Atlanta, while working on my doctorate, I had several conversations with him about issues of praxis in religious education. Although I never did get to know him well, I came to appreciate through those conversations his insights into the dynamics of double consciousness and his ability as an African American intellectual to mediate and negotiate the worlds of black and white.

Foster: We knew him as colleague and student. Bishop Thomas and Ethel Johnson, you knew him as friend as well as colleague. Tell us some stories about Grant so that we may begin to discern more clearly how his thinking about religious education developed.

Bishop Thomas: I first met Grant at Drew Theological Seminary in 1943 where we were both students. I had come from the South. I had attended a black college in the South and planned to return to South Carolina to be a rural pastor. He was from Philadelphia, had gone to Lincoln University, and planned to go on for a doctorate after completing his seminary degree. He was serving the great St. Mark's Methodist Church in New York as an assistant pastor at the time. Our friendship quickly bonded. We studied together and talked a lot. He was deeply concerned about our cultural roots—even before Alex Haley made the topic popular. He had a strong sense of his own heritage and family, and he thought deeply about the effects that segregation had on us. He wondered how I had survived. Grant was very serious. He knew he was at Drew for a deeper purpose. I don't think he ever had an errant idea. He was primarily interested in doing theology, and he was always planning to do a doctorate.

After we graduated I came back South and he stayed in the North, but our paths were to cross again soon. In 1947 I left a two-point charge in South Carolina to teach at Gammon Theological Seminary. At the same time Grant was asked to come to Clark College to be its chaplain. By then we were both married. Ruth and I had children and, at the time, they did not. Sometimes they would baby-sit for us. When we moved from Atlanta to Nashville to join the Board of Education of The Methodist Church, we knew we would continue visiting the Shockleys. That continued to be true through the years. Even though we both moved around a lot, we somehow always found a way back to each other's homes. When we moved to Nashville, he moved back to New York to work on his doctorate in religious education at Teachers College, Columbia University.

Ethel Johnson: I first knew Grant during those seminary years when he was the assistant pastor at St. Mark's Church. But we became friends and colleagues after his appointment to Janes Methodist Church in Brooklyn in 1953. Janes had at one time been a prominent white church, but as the neighborhood changed, it chose to close its doors in the 1940s rather than integrate. The annual conference reopened it in 1948 with two members—one black and one white. Grant was its third pastor. Ministry there was a great challenge.

I had joined this new congregation in 1949 while doing social work in Brooklyn. I soon became the congregation's parish visitor. After I graduated from Hartford Theological Seminary in 1954 Grant asked me to join the staff as the Director of Christian Education. The congregation may have had 100 members by then—all African American except for two white women. The neighborhood was both diverse and changing. The dominant economic group in the church was middle class, but the church served all of the people in the neighborhood. We had all kinds of programs—church school, after school programs, a day care center, basketball in the church gym. Much of our attention was directed to the community. The school system, for example, was not overly interested in the African American children attending the local schools. We decided as a congregation that we needed to look after our children. So we encouraged parents to be involved in the school. Part of my responsibility as the Director of Christian Education was to pay attention to the schools. If any of the children in the neighborhood had any concern about their experience at the school, they could come to the church.

Grant and I worked as a team. We would sit down and have long theological conversations. Benjamin Mays and Mordecai Johnson were key theological figures for us. Our conversations focused on what was the church—what was the goal of the church for African Americans both in and around the church. We both felt strongly that if the church were not involved in the community, our ministry was not relevant. At the same time the worship style, like that of St. Mark's, was "high church." St. Mark's sang the *venite* and the Psalms. Indeed, at times, St. Mark's seemed more Episcopalian than St. Phillip's nearby.

Grant brought this style with him. His approach to the leadership of worship was orderly and involved careful planning, which attracted the middle-income group from the neighborhood. He also had a deep appreciation of the spirituals—something that was not common in black churches at the time. Spirituals were included in worship, and he educated the congregation as to why they were important.

One other thing must be said. Grant always felt that African American people had to make a witness. He was never content to just sit back and let things go on around us. We had to be deeply involved. So he pushed me several times to do things I would never have otherwise done. For example, I never cared a thing about being a consecrated Christian educator, but Grant said we had to make a witness. This was not only a black and white issue. It also had to do with recognizing the importance of Christian education as a ministry of the church. He was a great champion for the church's education. So I went through the process in the annual conference to be consecrated. The conference had never had a consecrated certified Christian educator before. The bishop had no idea what consecration was. And when I had completed the process someone said that I could not be consecrated alone—it would look racist. So a longtime white director of Christian education was consecrated with me. As often happened, Grant had made his point, and in typical fashion, he acted behind the scene.

Foster: It is obvious that you had long and deep conversations with Grant. What did you talk about?

Bishop Thomas: Although the changing political and religious landscape of the nation influenced what we talked about, the themes were pretty consistent. In college we talked about politics in general, and church politics, specifically. Inevitably these discussions had to do with race. He wanted to know more about Atlanta, and I was interested in where he had been in the North. Even then he collected books on culture and race. We talked theology. Christology had to make a real difference for him. We talked a lot about worship. He couldn't stand liturgy that was random. Indeed, he didn't call it liturgy. We both talked about the Central Jurisdiction of The Methodist Church, which we both hated. And yet we could understand, given the training of the white mind in the South through centuries of slaveholding and later of segregation, how the church could make that decision. So we talked about race from within this cultural and historical perspective. We discovered in these conversations that although we appreciated the engagement of theology and culture, scholarship and social activism, he generally approached these issues as a theologian and I, as the social activist.

Smith: It is obvious from Grant's writings that education was a major theme in his work. He identified himself primarily as an educator—even when he was pastor, church bureaucrat and seminary and college president. What was it about education that kept his attention focused in this way?

Bishop Thomas: Part of his commitment to the possibilities in education may be traced back to his distrust of excessive emotion on the part of church leaders like Adam Clayton Powell. It was a critique we shared. In the first place, an emphasis on emotion could obscure the actual doubts that a thinking preacher has. Anyone who reads the Bible completely with affirmation has not really read the Bible. They haven't read Psalm 22 or Ecclesiastes or Lamentations. People in the Bible argued with God. They challenged God with questions. They doubted the presence and activity of God. We see it most profoundly in Jesus' protest, "My God, my God, why have you forsaken me?" Both of us detested being encouraged by the preacher to say "amen." We would say "amen" when we wanted to say "amen." The same with preachers who tell you to turn to your neighbor to say "I love you." I may like my neighbor, but don't tell me what to say. We were suspicious of excessive emotion because we wondered where the work of the Holy Spirit begins and our histrionics leave off. The issue for Grant was that he believed in loving God with all the mind. We both knew that many people had never heard an intelligent sermon from a black preacher. So his commitment to education was influenced, in part, by his desire for people to deliver sermons in good English, with a sound theology. This does not mean he discounted emotion. But he did insist on being responsible to the subject, and he advocated a nonmanipulative way of teaching in communicating with others about matters of Christian faith.

Ethel Johnson: He had two great loves: fulfilling the potential for all black people and the Christian education of all people. Christian education was for him the very foundation of what happens in the congregation. What the congregation does is absolutely important for children and their parents in developing values, nurturing self-worth, and deepening their understanding of their relationship to God. It did not matter the color of your skin or your social situation in life. For Grant, to be loved by God laid the foundation for loving self and neighbors.

Grant also believed that education had much to do with the human quest for freedom. Although we had often talked about the relationship of Christian education and freedom through the years, his thinking reached a new maturity in a presentation he made at the Methodist Theological School in Ohio in 1973. To be "free" for Grant included freedom in the person, with God, and from all the external things that surround us. Freedom ultimately had to do with our relationship with God. This relationship involved being engaged in the process of freedom and accepting the responsibility that comes with freedom by assuming leadership to ensure that all African American people are also lifted up into freedom.

It is at this point that we see something of his understanding of the relationship of Christian education and liberation. He always talked about Christian education as a part of liberation. Being educated to understand Christ frees one in any circumstance. But freedom brings with it responsibility. We are not free until everyone is free. To be free means to be agents of the freedom of others. This is why Grant wrote about being in the world to change the world. This view was seen in his ministry at Janes Church in the interdependence of worship and involvement in the community seven days of the week. A primary purpose of Christian education, in other words, was to free persons and, thereby, to free them to be agents of freedom for others.

Foster: This brings us to a theme we must discuss. How would you talk about Grant's view on race and the racism affecting the lives of African Americans during these years? We are aware that Jim Cone has given him the credit for first articulating the phrase "black theology." But how did he approach these issues?

Ethel Johnson: Grant really felt the pain of slavery. His feeling of this pain pushed him—and everyone else—to rise out of the legacy of slavery. He was not as deeply involved in the events of the Civil Rights Movement as were many of his peers. This had to do, in part, with his work with the Board of Missions of the Methodist Church that took him all over the globe. He simply was not in the United States much of the time. He may not have been in the forefront with proclamations, but he spoke freely and often to the issues in his speeches, class lectures, and sermons and witnessed consistently to the movement's importance through his relationships with people at all levels of church and academic life. He did the homework to understand the history of the situation. If you take at look at his book, *Heritage and Hope*, you get some feeling of the depth of his understanding of the experience of African Americans during that era, especially in the church. He did not jump quickly on the bandwagons of the movement. For example, it took him a while to move from "Negro" to "Black." We had always been called "Negro," and "Black" had always had a negative connotation to it when we were growing up. Once he adjusted to the possibilities in the word, however, he gave it his all.

Bishop Thomas: His approach to the issues of race and racism were highly educational, but that does not mean he was an apologist. Grant and I hated the whole system of segregation wherever it existed. We believed it could be rooted out—that someday people would understand it enough to end it. We talked a lot about the patterns and structures of racism. He would consistently bring a power analysis to the discussion—long before the post-modernists made the process popular. He would observe what was happening to both blacks and whites and could discern the advantages and privileges of whites in the structures and processes of institutions. He had the ability to see when either black or white leaders were being manipulative or coercive to get at their own ends.

Ethel Johnson: And yet, in all of these discussions we had, I never heard him put a person down. He would talk about different aspects of the experience. In some ways this is quite amazing, because he experienced discrimination in all its guises in so many direct and painful ways. The folk at the Methodist Board of Missions were brutal in their racism. Some denominational Board of Education staff members disparaged him and others blocked his efforts. Double consciousness was a heavy burden for all of us. In his work it was a double heavy burden.

Bishop Thomas: You mentioned that Grant came up with the phrase "Black Theology." He had a distinctive relationship to that movement. We knew back in the 1950s that someday someone would rebel against our immersion as black church leaders in white European theology. Jim Cone's book (*Black Theology and Black Power*) was inevitable. Grant would not have written this book. I would not have written it either. But we are glad that Cone did. We were very much in tune with what he had to say. We talked a lot about where the movement was taking us. We talked about the intransigence of the segregationists, of the Wallaces and the Faubuses. And we noted with surprise that it took a conservative Republican president to send the troops into Little Rock and to appoint Earl Warren to the Supreme Court.

Grant always urged us to keep this broader perspective on these issues. It's as if he were saying that God would raise up some people like Cone and King to do what Thomas and Shockley would not or could not do, and other people like Eisenhower to do what more liberal politicians would not or could not do. I can hear Grant now in these conversations. He would turn to me and say, "All right, Jim, now what do you think is going on here? Where is this taking us?" And we would then theorize about the meanings and the consequences of the events we were living through. In that conversation he would consistently remind us of the historical situation that led to these events and of the conditions in the place where they were being lived out. He was passionate about the importance of understanding the situation—of seeing it in its larger context.

Foster: This leads me to another question. During the last four or five years of Grant's life, I often felt that despite his preference for order and critical reflection, his anger over the conditions and consequences of racism was increasingly visible and more public. Was this something new? Or had our friendship deepened to the point that he was willing to share more of the depths of a motivating anger?

Bishop Thomas: His anger ran deep. I do think you are right. As his studies led him to a greater awareness of the history of racism, he became less inhibited in sharing the depths of his feelings. Let me put it this way. When Grant and I talked about the deep roots of racism, we did not even think of the word in the 1950s. We did not need to think of the word because the entity was so flagrant. You can't know the history of the roots of racism in this country without being angry. You know that anger can be expressed in a variety of ways and to several different ends. The prophets were angry. Grant's anger fed his passion toward education. For both of us it led to the necessity to demythologize history. When you think of the fact that the Voting Rights Act was passed a little more than thirty years ago, after 350 years of slavery, what are the proportions of that? When history says that from 1619 until 1965—by law, by subterfuge, by violence, by lynching—blacks were oppressed in this country, anyone who says that that kind of demon can be exorcised in thirty years or so, does not understand systems. All this is to say that you cannot know the history of racism without being angry.

Smith: This raises another question for me. Grant Shockley broke the color barrier many times through his professional life. He attended a predominantly white seminary. He served the only black congregation in a white annual conference of a predominantly white denomination. When he worked with the Board of Missions, black staff members in executive positions in denominational agencies were few and far between. He was the first black professor on the faculties of Garrett and Candler seminaries. While others marched he seemed to take up the challenge of breaking those racist barriers by assuming roles of leadership in institutions dominated by white folk. His approach as you describe him, always sounds as if he were the mediator, the one who stepped into a potentially dangerous and conflict-ridden situation in the quest to bring people together.

Bishop Thomas: I need to say a couple of different things here. First of all he and I did serve in predominantly black institutions—from black congregations, to, in Grant's case, black colleges and seminaries. In the second place, both of us have spent most of our lives in predominantly white institutional settings. Neither of us actively sought to be placed in these positions, but we did recognize that blacks and whites needed to have conversation with each other with integrity. This was not an easy decision, because black institutions also needed strong leadership. However, in the final analysis it meant in my case, joining the staff of the Board of Higher Education, and in Grant's case, accepting the invitation of church boards and white theological schools to be a part of their staffs and faculties. We often found ourselves to be the only black persons present at some meeting or conference or on some staff. We were constantly confronted with the paternalism of colleagues in these institutions. In those settings we traded on our performance—

our competence. We gave of ourselves 100 percent. We never went to anything unprepared. And we refused to respond to those experiences with some kind of reverse racism.

Ethel Johnson: We see another of his educational commitments here. Always he focused his attention on the importance of training others to be competent leaders. For Grant a key to progress in the racial struggles of the church and nation had to do with the development of leaders with the ability and skill to break through the institutional barriers that perpetuated racism, classism, and sexism. This was true in the congregation he served. We felt strongly about the quality of teaching that took place, so we developed a training program for teachers. He felt as strongly about the quality of leaders on church committees and community boards and agencies, and he provided programs of training for them. He paid little attention to income levels, racial identity, or social status in this regard. All people needed to be able to give leadership to the best of their ability and this meant providing them with the training so that they could perform in those roles competently. This emphasis ran through his work in national church agencies and on the faculties of the schools where he taught.

Bishop Thomas: I think I would add a more personal note to our conversation. Ethel, you and Chuck, have been the beneficiaries of Grant's friendship, as have I. He had a deep capacity for friendship. Every scholar does not. Maybe every scholar doesn't need it. But for Grant the values of loyalty and generosity were deeply rooted. He found it difficult to say anything critical about others. People always experienced him as a thoroughgoing gentleman. But it was deeper than that. He truly saw possibilities in others that they often did not see in themselves. This undoubtedly is the reason so many students—both black and white—viewed him to be one of their most important mentors. But it was also one of the reasons that he was able to mediate the dynamics of racism he encountered in church boards and academic institutions. And perhaps it is one of the reasons that he could see so clearly possibilities for the future of the church's education among all peoples in the distinctive features of the American black religious experience.

Smith: You have just provided a great transition to an exploration of the development of his thinking about the church's education through the lens of the black religious experience in North America.

SECTION I

A Way of Thinking About the Black Religious Education Experience

Introduction

Double Consciousness

Smith: One of Shockley's first published essays provides a clue to the framework for his thinking throughout his career. In "The Black Experience and Black Religion" he takes a stance among three contrasting views held by the black intellectual leadership after World War II seeking an appropriate response in the black community to white racism. Some, following the lead of Booker T. Washington, encouraged the black community to work with the white community for the benefit of the black world. Arguing against Washington, others shared with W. E. B. DuBois the view that the black community was necessarily involved in a struggle to move beyond the dynamics of oppression promulgated by a double consciousness in black self-identity. Still others followed Marcus Garvey, who did not so much reject the white world as promote the Black world. In this essay Shockley aligns himself with DuBois's view of the struggle among Black Americans for identity and self-worth.

Foster: In many ways Shockley shared DuBois's intellectual ability to move back and forth between black and white worlds—being in the white world while always conscious of being black. Like DuBois, he seized his own social location as the platform from which to make sense of the world in which he found himself. As a black Methodist

25

clergyman with deep ties to black church traditions and constituencies Shockley was, at the same time, a highly visible leader in the religious education establishment of an overwhelmingly European-American denomination. As an academic educated in black and white schools he served as faculty member and administrator in both white and black institutions of higher education. Shockley's sensitivity to the interactions of the black and white experience was nurtured in the experience of living at the border between them.

Smith: Booker T. Washington, Marcus Garvey, and W. E. B. DuBois articulated something of the range of options for living at those borders. They reflected in some measure the range of responses actually taken by Black Americans to the dynamics of racism, oppression, and injustice they encountered in American U.S. society. (1) Some members of the black community never left those communities to encounter directly the structures and customs of the dominant culture. (2) Some members lived within the black experience but interacted with the white culture for the benefit of the black community. They lived, in other words, as cultural brokers for other members of the black community. (3) Others were proponents of the black experience and self-reliance. Although members of this group held a range of perspectives on the meaning of the white experience, they focused their attention on promoting the black world and people. (4) Still another group lived on the edge of these two worlds—rooted in the black world while solidly footed in the white world. I like to compare the stance of those in this last group to that of Joseph in the court of the Pharaoh of Egypt. In that situation Joseph possessed the gifts and graces to live fully in the Egyptian world, but he used them to benefit his own people. Of these four approaches among oppressed peoples to a dominating culture, this last is undoubtedly the most precarious. Its adherents are the most vulnerable.

Foster: Shockley clearly embraced this last perspective. As a black clergyman in the Methodist Church he could easily find the fellowship he missed in the meetings of white clergy leaders among the black clergy and laity of segregated annual conferences and church meetings. As an academic in overwhelmingly white institutions of higher education he was typically the only black person present. His decision to be a professor of Christian education rather than of the theology he loved so

26

much contributed even more to the problems of his isolation and vulnerability in the academy.

Smith: His decision about how to live in this situation vocationally may be seen in this first essay. In it he lays the groundwork for an apology for the black experience that eventually becomes the interpretive framework for his writings on Christian education in the black experience. In choosing to follow the lead of DuBois he set before himself a daunting task. It meant writing for the black church and academic community *out of the experience* of that community to a white church and academic audience. This involved two sets of both/and thinking and writing—black and white; Christian educator (directed to the church) and theological educator (directed to the academy).

Contextuality

Foster: In the second essay in this section we find another clue to his way of thinking about the religious education of African American Christians. The decision to take the "twoness" of the black experience presented Shockley with a serious scholarly problem. In both the academic world and in popular culture, the sources to the white experience were readily and easily available. Sources to the experience of the descendants of the African diaspora received little overt attention. To be grounded in the black experience consequently meant he had to discover something of the roots of that experience in order to discern its distinctive character. The challenge before him centered on how to discover that which had been hidden or suppressed on the one hand, and to extricate on the other that which was distinctive from dominant white attitudes and perspectives. He used the word *contextual* to describe this effort. What were the contextual dynamics that shaped the black religious experience? He began his quest for the institutional and programmatic sources to this experience through the marginal comments and footnotes of church and educational historians. By turning to his colleagues in the academic and church worlds his attention was first focused on the role of white church and educational institutions in the development of black educational institutions and programs. Attention to the contribution of persisting African values and perspectives through the experience of slavery and segregation in the development of a black religious education came only later.

Smith: A second dimension in the context of black religious education for Shockley was the common experience of racism that dominated the consciousness of American blacks. Although a powerful and pervasive influence in black religious educational developments, this decision also reflected the lack of attention in the scholarly community at the time (indeed, the dismissal by the white scholarly community) to the indigenous sources of the black religious and educational experience. Not until well into the Civil Rights Movement did scholars turn in significant numbers to the exploration of the African cultural heritage of African Americans. Neither did they give much attention to the arts of the black community—either the folk art found in homes and churches or in the work of professional writers like Langston Hughes and Nora Thurston, musicians like Charles A. Tindley and Duke Ellington, and painters like Henry Ossawa Turner who did draw on indigenous black experience for themes and inspiration. The body of academic literature that now draws on the traditions of slave songs, stories and folk tales, quilts, and moral and religious instruction simply did not exist until late in Shockley's career. All this meant that he was not only often alone as a black man in the white academic and church cultures, he also lacked the resources and colleagues he needed to identify and articulate indigenous black religious and educational traditions and patterns.

Foster: Again we can begin to see in the way he approached the quest for the contextual roots of the black religious education experience, something of the influence of double consciousness in his own thinking. Until his later writings he does not look for the origins of the black religious experience in Africa but begins instead with the African's experience of slavery in North America. This decision meant that his quest led him to focus attention on the experience of African Americans in the religious education institutions of the dominant white culture. In this regard he tended to follow the dominant educational historiography of his own graduate school days that limited the study of education to the influence of schooling. This meant that he did not look for indigenous sources to that experience or for ways in which African cultural sources contributed to the creative efforts of

28

slaves to humanize their conditions generally or to liberate themselves from the shackles of their bondage.

Smith: As we consider the development of his thought it is important to observe that initially the heritage of the African diaspora functioned passively. The experience of double consciousness was too close. As someone aware of the bind of African Americans seeking to understand themselves without reference to the dominant white culture, his own theoretical framework does not remove that bind for his readers. This second essay however, is an important step in the evolution toward an awareness of the constructive contributions of that African heritage to the development of the black religious experience and of its significance for the religious education of all Christians. It does make evident the terrible constraints within which the emerging black Christian religious education consciousness was formed in the United States.

Foster: Even as we recognize the limitations in the original framework with which he approached the exploration of the sources to religious education in the black church, his research brought to the attention of a woefully ignorant church leadership in both white and black churches the institutional history of black religious education. It may be hard for some to realize that in 1974 his research was experienced by many black Christians as liberating. Invariably he was besieged by requests for copies of his lectures and notes by people who wanted to share his findings with friends and colleagues. It may be as difficult for some to realize that many white readers of that same period were equally offended by his descriptions of the racism in their church heritages and his insistence upon the importance of black historical self-consciousness.

Double Consciousness

The following excerpt has been taken from an essay by Grant S. Shockley entitled "The Black Experience and Black Religion," which appeared in *The Black Church* 2 (1974), pages 94-97. In it Shockley describes the notion of double consciousness that provided the interpretive lens through which he explored the sources to the black religious experience.

Black Experience

Being Black in the United States of America is a peculiar experience. It is a highly problematic existence in both its personal and social dimensions. Being Black is a problem of being different because of the color of one's skin and the texture of one's hair. In America where the overwhelming majority of people are of white complexion, being Black is a color problem. B. L. Putnam Weale in his *The Conflict of Color* states:

> There is perhaps nothing quite so cruel in the whole world as the strange law which has given to so many scores of millions of human beings coal-black faces and bodies, thus so distinguishing them from the rest of the human family that this singular colour . . . is held to be the mark of the beast. . . . But in the two Americas . . . the coal-black native is almost considered as a man utterly separated from the rest of the world's inhabitants, and therefore not far removed from being accursed.[1]

The black experience in America is not only problematic because of the "high visibility of color." Being black in a white-oriented and white-dominated society imputes inferiority to non-whiteness. Impotent to refute this assignment and its consequent humiliations in any significant way, Black people became, and in many ways remain, the victims of discrimination and segregation with subsequent inferior social, economic, political, cultural, and educational status.

Such a situation involves the constant necessity to reconcile two conflicting if not separate identities. On the one hand, Black people, recognizing their human identity which is shared with all other members of the species, naturally seek and expect the response that should be normal for all who share a common humanity. Specifically, Black people expect acceptance as members of the human family, security of persons, respect of persons, equal opportunity, freedom, etc. On the other hand, Black people in America have found it necessary, often for their very survival, to respond to a white conceptualized identity "for" Black people which, wittingly or unwittingly, dehumanizes, depersonalizes, desocializes, and disempowers. This anomalous situation, faced to a greater or lesser degree in America by all persons of any visible Black African ancestry, has engendered in the psyche of Black people a highly articulated self-consciousness—often a hypersensitivity but invariably a sense of dual existence. W. E. B. DuBois in his *The Souls of Black Folk* calls it "twoness": "One ever feels his twoness,—an American, a Negro; two souls, two

30

thoughts, two unreconciled strivings; two warring ideals in one dark body, whose dogged strength alone keeps it from being torn asunder."

This is the Black experience—"the life and world of any and all people of color who must or will identify themselves as being of African descent." It is "the ever present reality of knowing and feeling and living as a non-white in a white-oriented and white-controlled society. It is the Black group experience, historic and present, of being oppressed, deprived, excluded, alienated and rejected."[2]

The implications of the "Black experience" for religious education derives not only from the fact that the earliest attitudes held toward Blacks were, almost without exception, at best paternalistic and at worst racist, but also from the fact that through it all Black people demonstrated the capacity to hold these two estimations in tension, selecting from the white Christian model presented to them in a perverted fashion that which was necessary for survival as persons and rejecting that which sought to destroy every vestige of their self-worth and respect.

Black Religious Experience

The plight of the Black American, who according to J. Saunders Redding *"lives constantly on two planes of awareness,"* was not only one of personal rejection but also one of social and religious segregation. Winthrop D. Jordan wrote in *White over Black*: "The Negro's color sets him radically apart from Englishmen. It also served as a highly visible label identifying the natives of a distant continent which for ages Christians had known as a land of men radically defective in religion."[3]

Several significant implications for religious education among Black people derive from this "splitness" or double-visioned perspective which caused J. Saunders Redding to say that the Black American *"lives on two planes of awareness."* This dual existence influenced their religious development historically and presently. It was and is the existential situation in which Black theological belief systems developed. In their sermons, spirituals, prayers, and Sunday school teachings, Black people came to terms with their blackness, their expressional gifts, and their social situation of slavery and brutalizing oppression in a white-racist church and society. There is where they "worked out their salvation" in relation to questions of their bondage, their separation from family, their chattel status, their idea of good and evil, of God and satan. From its beginning in the time of slavery, the church came to have a particular significance for Black people because it provided them with a "gathered community" of relative freedom, expressional outlet, community information, group solidarity, personal affirmation, mutual aid, and leadership development.

The Black community, then more than now probably, grew up around and was influenced by the Black Church more than any other single institution. As a central meeting place, a platform for the promulgation of ideas, a likely place to hear of a job, a basic meeting place for youth, and an educational institution, it was practically unrivaled as a center of power. Further, because little attention was given to the moral and ethical development of Black people by any other institution prior to emancipation, the large influence of the church in this area must be regarded as singular. In short, the church was the first institution in the Black community to deal seriously with the split-identity crisis of the comprehensive black-white dichotomy in American society. The experience of the antebellum black Church with the problem of "twoness" is another area from which implications for religious education may be drawn.

Black churches in free states and territories before and after the Civil War were generally the most likely centers of protest against slavery and advocates of civil rights for the Black community. In the Pre–Civil War slave states, Black churches tended in many instances to surface those elements of character which enabled survival and a measure of security. Even in the darkest periods the Black "invisible church" produced insurrectionists such as Gabriel Prosser, Denmark Vesey, and Nat Turner. Also, the "free" Black church in the South before emancipation made a significant contribution to the education of slaves and free people of color. It is significant that this historical Black preacher and Black church provided the kind of preaching, worship, activities, and program which supported our people in their groping efforts to affirm their identity, worth, and aspirations as human beings and children of God. In that earlier situation the church was educator. What is its role today in dealing with the "twoness" in the Black church and community?

Contextuality

In the following excerpt from an essay entitled "Christian Education and the Black Church: A Contextual Approach" (*Journal of the Interdenominational Theological Center* 2 [1974], pages 75-85), Shockley begins the daunting task of uncovering elements of the formal educational experience of Black Americans sponsored by Christian churches. Three categories identified in this essay continued to frame his thinking about that history for the rest of his career: religious education as socialization into the life of the church, religious education as the mission of the church, and black initiatives responsive to the racism encountered in the church's education. His attention, consequently, was drawn to the institutional and sociocultural experience of blacks in America.

Introduction

Christian educators in the black church are beginning to recognize some new issues involved in defining their taste. Primary among these questions are not only the standard ones of objectives, content, curriculum, learning, teaching, leadership, and evaluation, but the more insistent and crucial question of the relationship of these to the black experience, the black community, the black church, black theology, and black liberation. In other words, the new questions for Christian education as they are viewed by the black church are essentially contextual. From goal-setting to evaluating, black educators in black churches are viewing the educational process in relation to the kind of learning and teaching that considers the black experience as central and the liberation of black people as its focal point. Briefly, then, the new definition of Christian education views it as that process which teaches concepts, attitudes, and skills which facilitate meaningful learning in relation to the black experience and the church's implicit taste of humanization and liberation.

The new definition of Christian education in relation to the black church is not ephemeral. It has a long and deep history. The main outline of that history must be understood if black church members are to be involved meaningfully in the task of liberation in the black church through Christian education. The purpose of this paper, then, is to review that history and to suggest some implications it may have for the theory, practice, and design of Christian education in black churches in America.

Historical Background

The earliest efforts toward the Christian education of blacks in America grew out of and centered around Christian evangelization and missions.

There are indications of intention and deed regarding the Christian education of blacks on the part of both Puritans and Anglicans in the first quarter of the seventeenth century. "As early as 1620, when the slave trade began, English clergymen had expressed an interest in extending religious training to those in bondage beyond the seas and had made some progress in this direction."[4]

In 1624, Anthony Johnson, one of the twenty indentured African servants brought to America in 1619, and his wife, Isabell, became the parents of the first black child to be born in "English" America. The child, a boy, was taken to the Anglican church in Jamestown (Virginia) where he was christened "William" in the faith of his parents. It is reasonably certain these black parents were catechized prior to, or during, that Baptism.[5]

Father White (Jesuit) brought two West Indian Negroes (Sousa Mathias and Francisco) with him as personal servants when he came to America (Virginia) in 1634. In all likelihood both of these servants had been Baptized prior to their arrival here and had been given informal instruction by their masterpriest.[6]

Prior to the institutionalization of chattel slavery which began in Virginia as early as 1667, many examples of Christian education of this kind can be found.

With the rise and spread of chattel slavery the situation alters radically. Whereas previously both Baptism and instruction were available routinely, the question of Baptizing slaves raised the issue of their status as Baptized Christians in relation to their condition of servitude.

Here the churches compromised both the civil and spiritual rights of the slave by equivocating over the meaning of Baptism and adulterated the content of his religious instruction. For an example, on the issue of slavery, neither the Church nor the Virginia colonists objected when the Virginia Assembly declared: "Baptism doth not alter the condition of the person as to his bondage or freedom: that divers masters, freed from this doubt, may more carefully endeavour the propagation of Christianity."[7]

Between 1619 and 1666 Baptism and Christian education were available somewhat as ends in themselves. After 1667 they were to be means to the end of maintaining the institution of slavery and placating the conscience of the Church. While this situation was not without some "benefit" to the slave (for example, it obtained literacy for many), it also corrupted the church's judgment and compromised her power in dealing with her larger future responsibilities to blacks.

Black Enslavement and Christian Education Missions: 1667–1863

While Christian education among black people in America antedates any other organized effort to improve the slave's condition of chattel servitude and illiteracy, these educational experiences were generally truncated to meet the requirements of slavemasters. They were also held on a segregated basis.

ANGLICAN-PROTESTANT EPISCOPAL

The first major missionary effort directed toward the elevation of the status of blacks in America was that of the Society for the Propagation of the Gospel in Foreign Parts (1701). It was founded for the purpose of "supplying the destitution of religious institutions and privileges among the inhabitants of the North American colonies . . . and . . . of extending the Gospel to the Indian and Negroes."[8]

Missionaries from this Society evangelized and taught among blacks from 1702 to 1819 along the Eastern seaboard from New England to South Carolina.

Following the Revolutionary War mission Christian education work shifted to the local parishes of Protestant Episcopal Churches where scores of rectors conducted "colored Sunday Schools" as a regular part of their parish activities.

ROMAN CATHOLIC

Between the introduction of chattel slavery and slave emancipation thousands of black slaves had become Roman Catholics. The Catholic treatment of slaves, generally, and their education was unique. Unlike most Protestant groups, who conceived of conversion and education as means toward developing a more efficient quasi-human labor machine, Catholics viewed conversion and education more as ends in themselves. In keeping with this, Catholic treatment of slaves was, generally, somewhat more humane. Much of their religious instruction was received in the homes of their masters, where they were thought of as "the family" or "our family." Rarely were black Catholic families separated or sold without each other.

Christian instruction was given to slave workers on the plantations and to free blacks in the Negro "settlements." From the very beginning, Sunday schools were established for both free and servant blacks to supplement their secular education. Such classes usually met on Sunday afternoon or during the week.

CONGREGATIONAL

The great Puritan divine, Cotton Mather favored both the conversion and baptism of slaves. Together with John Eliot, he also favored religious instruction for them. Richard Baxter in a tract published in London in 1673 is found in agreement with Eliot and Mather.

Stewart found in the middle of the nineteenth century that the religious education of Blacks in Connecticut Congregationalism "had increased and their instruction in matters of religion was an affair of importance."[9]

LUTHERAN

From the earliest years of the nineteenth century, Lutherans in America manifested an interest in the Christian education of blacks. Sunday Schools for blacks were found to have been related to their churches in both the North and South. Of course, these facilities were used on a segregated basis.

THE SOCIETY OF FRIENDS

Instances of Quaker missionary Christian education activity among blacks are fairly numerous. The women of the Maryland Society protested the lack of education for black children in 1678. In 1679 and again in 1690, George Fox writes to America, "And, also, you must teach and instruct blacks and Indians."[10] The Philadelphia Yearly Meeting required Christian education for their slaves, "during the time they have for them." Anthony Benezet began his evening school for the religious and secular instruction of blacks in 1750. Black Quaker, Paul Cuffe, opened his school for blacks in Massachusetts about this same time. In North Carolina (1815) Quakers were still advocating literacy and religious instruction for blacks. The Society of Friends never attracted large numbers of black worshipers, however, despite their liberal stand and willingness to educate blacks in religion.

PRESBYTERIAN

Virginia Presbyterians initiated efforts toward the religious education of blacks as early as 1747 through the ministry of Samuel Davies and John

Todd.[11] Presbyterians were also among the first major religious denominations to advocate education for blacks after their emancipation. In 1800 the General Assembly recommended "the instruction of Negroes, in various parts of the country, who were destitute of the means of grace." The United Presbyterians began a rigorous Mission Sunday School Program in the South in 1890 out of which came more than 3,800 Sunday Schools and churches.

MORAVIAN

One of the few religious denominations that came to America, primarily, to evangelize were the Moravians. About 1735 they organized a congregation consisting of Indians and blacks as well as white settlers. In 1738 we find the Moravians attempting to organize missions for blacks. The principal activity in these missions was religious instruction. Nathanael Seidel and Eric Westman itinerated west of the Susquehanna River in the winter of 1747. Later they made their way to Virginia where they catechized and evangelized blacks. In 1749 in Philadelphia, blacks sought out the Moravians for instruction and baptism. Blacks attended the "black" chapel and Sunday School built for them in Salem, North Carolina in 1823. In 1865 the Moravians founded a mission among the emancipated blacks with a "flourishing Sunday School."[12]

METHODIST

Methodist concern for the Christian education of blacks is evidenced in a General Conference Journal entry in 1785. In answer to the question "What can be done in order to instruct poor children, white and black, to read?" The answer was, "Let us labor, as the heart of one man, to establish Sunday Schools, in or near the place of public worship."

In 1785 William Elliott is said to have founded Methodist Sunday Schools in Virginia, one for blacks and one for whites. A Sunday School was held in the home of Thomas Crenshaw (Virginia) in 1786. John Charleston, later to become an outstanding African Methodist Episcopal minister, attended the Crenshaws' school. In 1787 George Daughty, a Methodist preacher, was drenched with water at the public pump for conducting a Sunday school including blacks. An "African Sunday School" existed in New York about 1817. It had possibly been promoted by the black Methodists, probably those who became AME Zions.[13]

Blacks and the Sunday School Movement

The Sunday School Movement in America never effectively related itself to black people. The bulk and center of Protestant education has never shown more than a token interest in comprehensive nonsegregated education, nor has it ever really come to terms with its white racism. It is interesting to trace this development.

The vast majority of English and other missionaries serving in America withdrew at the close of the Revolutionary War. This left the missionizing and evangelizing of blacks (and Indians) to the emerging American denominations. While there was no lack of enthusiasm to continue the work of organizations such as the Society for the Propagation of the Gospel, the direction of this American development in the area of Christian education in relation to blacks moved toward segregated Sunday Schools.

There are further distressing developments in the Sunday School Movement in relation to blacks. A high degree of sensitivity and concern on the part of some white patrons of Sunday Schools of blacks for the possible consequence of slaves learning more than the restricted and innocuous biblical material requisitioned in this period is mirrored in Carter G. Woodson's observation: "The colored pauper children apprenticed by church wardens were prohibited by statute immediately after Gabriel's (Prosser) Insurrection in 1800."[14]

Still another example is W. E. B. DuBois's report, in connection with the black revolt under Toussaint L'Overture in Haiti, that South Carolina passed a law declaring:

> It shall not be lawful for any number of slaves, free Negroes, mulattoes, or mestizoes, even in the company of white persons to meet together and assemble for the purpose of mental instruction or religious worship, either before the rising of the sun or the going down of the same.[15]

Levi Coffin's Sunday School also upset a number of slaveholders. Again Woodson reports:

> In 1821 certain masters were sending their slaves to a Sunday School opened by Levi Coffin. . . . Before the slaves had learned more than to spell words of two or three syllables, masters became unduly alarmed, thinking that such instruction would make the slaves discontented.[16]

Despite the racially bigoted character of the Sunday School in the post-Revolutionary years, it still must be emphasized that it was an important factor in Negro education. Woodson reminds us of this: "Although cloaked with the purpose of bringing the blacks to God by giving them religious instruction the institution (Sunday Schools) permitted its workers to teach them reading and writing when they were not allowed to study such in other institutions."[17]

ORAL INSTRUCTION PERIOD

The objective of the American Sunday School Union's "Mississippi Valley Enterprise," launched in 1830 was "to organize a Sunday School within two years, in every destitute place in the Valley of the Mississippi." This "Enterprise" never reached blacks. As a matter of fact between 1830 and 1890 little or nothing was done for the religious education of Negroes in the Mississippi Valley, despite the fact that this section comprised one of the most densely populated black areas in the country.

This "by-pass" was characteristic of the operational style of the A.S.S.U., particularly during the slavery era. Lawrence Jones suggests the reason for this as he speaks about the A.S.S.U. as well as the American Tract Society and the American Bible Society and their defections from the Abolition Movement. "These groups were charged with ignoring the whole issue of slavery in order not to alienate those slave holders who offered financial support."[18]

The main thrust and dominant motif in the Christian education that was offered to blacks during slavery and especially from 1800 onward was not "religious" or "Christian" basically, but rather sub-Christian and racist.

Blacks were prohibited by the "black codes" from gathering or being gathered together as a group to learn to read or write; therefore, much Christian education from about 1834 onward was relegated to what Woodson calls "religion without letters" or oral (catechetical) instruction.

The most widely used of these catechisms was the one developed by William Capers (1790–1855). In reality it was a theology of black dehumanization, as seen in this example:

Q. What did God make man out of?
A. The dust of the ground.
Q. What does this teach you?
A. To be humble.[19]

The slave was not only taught to be "humble" but he was also taught that slavery could be justified. In Caper's catechism the slave read that God "sentenced" man to "labor and sorrow, pain and death." This is a significant modification of its source—John Wesley's catechism, which read that mankind was "driven out of paradise and became subject to pain and death."

THE NADIR

Following the Emancipation of the slaves (1863), the conclusion of the Civil War (1865), and the Reconstruction Era (1866–1876), black Sunday schools were generally neglected, especially in the South. What energy and church funds that were available were put into secular schools for the ex-slaves, forming the foundation for a system of denomination-ally related black colleges. Christian (parish) education was left largely to Northern missionaries or to the black churches that were missionizing in the then "liberated" South. Some few black Sunday Schools were even united with local and state Unions in this period, especially in the larger urban centers of the North.

Generally speaking, however, the time between 1863 and 1893 repre-sented a low point in Christian (parish) education among blacks insofar as the A.S.S.U. and the white denominations were concerned.

INTERNATIONAL SUNDAY SCHOOL ASSOCIATION ERA

In 1893 the International Sunday School Convention meeting in St. Louis, Missouri, took an action that created a field-secretariat approach to Sunday School Missions. Between 1895 and 1908 four pioneer black reli-gious educators traveled throughout the South promoting black Sunday Schools and training leaders, particularly in areas where none existed. These men were L. B. Maxell, Silas X. Floyd, G. B. Marcus, and James E. Shepherd.

About this time other denominations, especially the Methodists, Episcopalians, and Baptists, created denominational field staff positions in the area of Sunday School and in some cases youth work.

The inability of the local black Sunday School Associations to raise their part of the budget for the International Sunday School Association plan caused it to fail.

THE CLIFTON PLAN

In search of a more feasible plan to improve Christian Education among blacks, W. N. Hartshorn, President of the International Sunday school Association called together a group of leading religious educators and Sunday School workers at his summer home in Massachusetts in

1908. The 1908 Clifton Conference is notable because it was the first such meeting that included blacks to discuss and solve "their" problem of Christian education.

The "Clifton Plan," produced at this conference, envisioned courses in religious education and Sunday School administration in the black colleges whose students and graduates would train black lay teachers and Sunday School workers in local leadership training type courses.[20]

SUMMARY

Early efforts toward the Christian education of blacks grew out of the mission impulse. This motive was subverted by the equivocation of the churches on the issue of the human and political rights of chattel slaves.

Christian education among blacks antedates any other organized effort to improve the slave's condition of illiteracy. Much education so received however, was a truncated version of the biblical message accommodated to the requirements of slaveholders. It also assumed black intellectual inferiority.

The (white) Sunday School Movement did not relate itself to blacks in helpful or effective ways. It showed only token interest in integrated schools and failed consistently to come to terms with its racist policies and practices.

Black Church Movements and Christian Education

The mainlines of Christian education development in black denominations which originated in the early part of the nineteenth century become highly instructive as we view the current task of Christian education in the black church. Representing as they did separatism occasioned by racial prejudice and discrimination rather than disputes over doctrine, liturgy, or polity, they perceived rather early the incompatibility of the "white over black" attitude of their fellow Christians and opted for a separate development approach. This approach had considerable viability at its beginning, and it continued into the present century. Presently it serves as a launching model for contextual learning in black churches generally.

A.M.E.

In 1795 Richard Allen, the founder and the first Bishop of the African Methodist Episcopal Church established in 1816, organized the first black

(Church related) Sunday School in America. Charles S. Smith organized the first black Sunday School Union in 1882 and in 1888 became one of the first Black Christian Education executives as Corresponding Secretary of the Union. W. H. Coleman conducted the first Black Leadership Training Enterprise in 1874 while youth work in the form of Christian Endeavor societies started early in the 1880s. Adult work had begun in the 1850s as literary societies. By the 1920s the denomination had a comprehensive, national program of Christian education.

A.M.E. Church literature, "the First . . . ever published in this country for the exclusive use of Negro Sunday Schools"[21] has been published since the 1800s. In 1936 a Board of Religious Education was established to coordinate Sunday Schools, Allen Christian Endeavor Societies, and Leadership Education programs. In 1952 this Board became the Division of Christian Education of the General Board of Education.

A.M.E. ZION

Christian education in the form of Sunday School work was organized in A.M.E. Zion Churches along the Eastern seaboard and as far west as Pittsburgh a generation prior to the Civil War.[22] A Sunday School Union was founded in 1889. In 1916 the A.M.E. Zion General Conference elected a General Superintendent of Sunday Schools and an Editor of Sunday School literature, and created a Sunday School Board. In the 1880s the Varick (Youth) Christian Endeavor Society was organized. Adult education, as in the A.M.E. Zion Churches, began in the form of literacy societies in the 1860s.

Scant records about the first publication of Sunday School and youth literature in the A.M.E. Zion Church indicate that it got underway about 1876, prior to which time it probably used Methodist Episcopal materials.

In 1924 the General Conference combined the Sunday School and Christian Endeavor Department forming the Department of Religious Education. In 1932 this was merged with the Department of Education to create the Christian Education Department, the name of which was later changed to the Board of Christian Education.

C.M.E. (1870)

Sunday Schools existed in the C.M.E. Church prior to its organization as a denomination in 1870. They were organized into a department in 1928. An Epworth League Department was organized in 1902. In 1934 these departments were merged to form the General Board of Religious

Education. Between 1934 and 1938 the youth of the denomination were organized, and in 1950 the General Conference Board of Education was merged with the Board of Religious Education to form the General Board of Christian Education.

The curriculum materials used in the C.M.E. Church are adapted versions of the materials in the United Methodist Church.

BAPTIST (1880)

Baptist Sunday Schools had existed among blacks since the 1770s. James D. Tyms, in his volume *The Rise of Religious Education Among Negro Baptists*,[23] places the beginnings of a denomination-wide organized Christian Education among black Baptists in 1895 when the National Baptist Educational Convention met in Atlanta, Georgia. Following an internal struggle respecting the control of writing, editing, printing, and publishing printed resources for Baptist Sunday Schools, etc. a National Baptist Publishing Board was established in Nashville under black management. Other administrative program units of the National Baptist Convention, Inc. were The Sunday School Congress and The Baptist Young People's Union Board, later the Baptist Young People's Training Union (B.Y.P.U.).

In 1915 The Convention divided. The National Baptist Convention, Inc. organized the National Sunday School and B.Y.P.U. Congress, a merger of the former Sunday School Board and National B.Y.P.U. boards.

Section II

Sources for a Liberative Religious Education

Introduction

Smith: Within the framework of double consciousness and the contextual history of African Americans in the United States, Shockley began to develop a way of thinking about religious education in the black experience. Sources to his thinking are evident in the four essays that follow. As an academic he drew heavily on the scholarship of the Civil Rights and Black Power Movements, especially the new writings in Black Theology. As a student of popular culture he drew insights from an extensive collection of articles on the quests of peoples around the globe for freedom and civil rights from newspapers and magazines he had begun collecting during his travels as the Secretary of Christian Education of the Board of Missions of the Methodist Church. Through this work he was also introduced to leaders of the political movements for independence in colonial countries and to liberation theologians and educators recasting the categories of European theology and education through the experience of the oppressed.

Foster: His international travel placed his reflections on the Black American quest for civil rights into a larger global context. This is most evident in the first essay that follows. Encounters with Christian activists in colonial or newly independent nations from Asia and Africa deepened his understanding of the human quest for freedom and provided him with a new vocabulary to describe an agenda for black church religious education. Paulo Freire, the Brazilian educator, and Rubem Alves, the Methodist liberation theologian from South

America, in particular, influenced his reading of the goals and strategies of both the Civil Rights and Black Power Movements and reinforced his support for Black Theology as the distinctively American liberation perspective on the human quest for freedom from oppression. In this essay he sets the frame for a global and pluralist perspective on the educational efforts of Christian communities.

Smith: The second and third selections provide an overview of Shockley's engagement with the interplay of liberation and black theologies in his quest for a way of thinking about the contribution of black religious education to our understanding of Christian religious education. Written about twenty years apart they illumine the development of his thinking about the mutuality of liberation and Black Theology in religious education. In the first place he identifies himself clearly with the developments in Black Theology and thereby with the causes of the Black Power Movement. Second, he locates those developments in the larger human quest for freedom especially as articulated through the work of Freire and the liberation theologians of South America and the indigenous theologians of Africa. Third, he is deeply conscious of the fact that his audience has contrasting expectations for his discussion of black church religious education. For his predominantly white audience he is interpreter of the interplay of Black and Liberation Theologies. For professional religious educators, he is apologist for Black Theology and the Black American quest for freedom in the Civil Rights Movement. For black church women and men, he is also advocate for the contribution of the black experience in religious education to the church's quest for justice in a world of oppression and domination.

Foster: In this regard we return to a theme we have already mentioned. Even as he sought to make his larger church and academic audience aware of the distinctive contributions of Black Theology to the larger theological and education conversations, his context continued to be that of the dominant white church. Even as he explicates the sources to a religious education grounded in Black Theology perspectives, he still had not asked to what extent black churches really wanted an education embodying values and perspectives inherited from Europe. Again we can see the persistence of double consciousness in his scholarly quest. Even as he advocates for the contribution of Black

Theology to our understanding of religious education between 1976 and 1995, he does not quite break out of the religious educational box inherited from Europe. He continues to think about education in categories drawn from European traditions of schooling with their particular understandings of curriculum, teaching, and learning. Despite his appreciation for Freire's understanding of praxis in education, he continues to develop a model of religious education that begins with theory or theology and moves to practice. Despite a deep appreciation for the African heritage and the cultural, religious, and theological resources of African Americans that he believed enhanced and enriched the religious education experience of all peoples, the measure of what is educational, in other words, drew on its European antecedents. After his retirement he was invited to teach at the Candler School of Theology and Clark Atlanta University where he increasingly turned his attention to an exploration of the African sources to that religious education experience that had persisted in the black church experience despite dominant white culture efforts to suppress or extinguish them.

Perhaps as important as the shift taking place in his thinking during his latter years is our own discovery, while working through his writings, of the persistence in his quest to disentangle himself from the bind of double consciousness in his work. In that effort he provides a powerful lens into the intellectual journey of a scholar seeking to develop a black perspective on religious education that functions as a full partner in the discussions of the field. Shockley's awareness of this shift may be most evident in the fourth essay in this section. In a paper presented to a conference at the Methodist Theological School in Ohio in 1985, he makes explicit for the first time his conviction that the tasks of discovering and creating a black christian education are crucial for the religious education in black churches and among all Christians.

Smith: That quest to disentangle himself from the bondage of double consciousness however, was not to be an easy one. A double message persists in these essays. On the one hand his interpretation of the black religious education experience conveys the message that religious education is good and the black church should embrace it. But on the other hand he documents over and again ways in which the formal religious education experience of black Christians has not been good for the health of the black church or its members. In the evolution of Shockley's intellectual life his awareness of this sense of being "caught" in the net of double consciousness evolves over time. So in the essays that follow he identifies sources in the black church tradition that make its advocates and interpreters full partners in the conversations about the education of all Christians. At the same time he articulates ways in which dominant approaches to religious education experience have not been fully beneficial to the well-being of the black community. He illustrates again in this dichotomy something of his ability to sit at the edge of the worlds of two different peoples whose lives have been inextricably intertwined, without removing the bind of double consciousness on the one "partner" who has suffered much from the other. It is at this point that Shockley's personal journey to full awareness of the double consciousness in his own intellectual pursuits functions paradigmatically for the gradual emancipation from that bind that is probably typical of most of us—both black and white.

Transcendence and Mystery in the Third World

The following essay was published in a collection edited by Earl D. C. Brewer and entitled, *Transcendence and Mystery* (New York: IDOC/America, Inc., 1973), pages 76-88. In it Shockley expands the frame of reference for his thinking about black church religious education from the vantage point of the liberation movements around the world and within the larger concerns of religious education among the religions of the world.

Societies, no less than persons, have a capacity for transcendence. In examining the relationship of transcendence, mystery, and society, we raise several questions. What are the meanings of transcendence, mystery, and Third World? What are the impact and direction of transcendence and mystery? And what are the implications and probabilities for the first and second worlds as well as the Third World?

Definitions

Transcendence. The phenomenon of transcendence can be defined from the perspective of the experience itself or from the perspective of the experiencer. As an experience, it can be said to be one of mystery, otherness, beyondness, or ultimacy. From the standpoint of the experiencer, it suggests a religion, a philosophy, a theology or lifestyle based on that experience.[1]

Mystery. A mystery is an uncomprehended knowledge or truth, a humanly insoluble problem, an unclarified and unclarifiable phenomenon. Michael B. Foster says that E. L. Mascall defines a mystery by distinguishing it from a problem and a puzzle:

> A problem is something that can be solved, and which ceases to be mysterious when it is solved. Mystery is something fundamentally different. . . . A puzzle is like a problem in that it looks mysterious but is not. The apparent mystery is dispelled in this case, not by acquiring further knowledge, but by clarification of what we know already. . . . But for the Christian theologian there must be a third thing also, namely, mysteries, which remain mysterious even when understood, because, though understood, they exceed our comprehension.[2]

For the purposes of this paper transcendence and mystery will be interchangeable terms. Either may pertain to that idea or thing or being that "stands over against" the known experience or the known subject—more simply, the "more than" aspect of existence.

The Third World. This "cant" term has appeared in the literature of geopolitics since the late 1950s. Derived from the French *tiers monde*, it originally referred to the nations that were non-Communist and non-Western. J. D. B. Miller, in *The Politics of the Third World*,[3] indicates that it has three characteristics: non-European, non-Communist, poor. For his purposes, the Third World consists of such nations in Africa and Asia.[4] Strangely, he omits Latin America. His reasons for doing so are (1) its colonies received their independence more than a century ago; (2) its predominant culture is Latin, that is, Spanish and Portuguese, not Indian; and (3) its controlling powers were European.

These reasons and others, however, are precisely why we will include Latin America in the Third World. Though most of her countries received political independence years ago, they are still economically and in other ways "colonial." While the predominant ethos of many Latin American countries is "Latin," the culture of the indigenous populations is Indian. The fact that the controlling powers in Latin America are European is not only the reason for much of the poverty and second-class status of the people and nations, but also the proof that Europeans have robbed nationals of their power.

"Bandungia"[5] is another term that has been used for the Third World. For Vera Micheles Dean, Bandungia (after Bandung, Indonesia, where the first Afro-Asian conference took place in 1955) represents those areas of the world that followed rather than led in moving from the pre-industrial to the industrial era. Her comment on this point is pertinent:

> For a variety of reasons, recorded in history, this vast land stopped developing politically, economically, and socially around 1400 (A.D.) just about the same time that the Western nations started on a period of extraordinary growth with the age of exploration and colonial expansion, the Renaissance, the Reformation, the English, French and American revolutions and the Industrial Revolution. As a result, Bandungia entered the twentieth century with those institutions and practices not very different from those it had four or five centuries before.[6]

This interpretation, then, would refer to Western Europe as the "first" world. North America would be considered the "second" world, while African and Asian countries that attended Bandung would be the Third World.

While no Latin American Countries attended Bandung, Dean seems to include them as de facto members, principally because of their retardation in economic development: "This land of Bandungia is peripatetic. It is found in Asia, in Africa, in the Middle East, in Latin America and something like it existed in Eastern Europe before 1939."[7] Hensman defines the Third World as a politicized movement toward liberation,

> marked by the emergence of a highly developed political consciousness, social dynamism, and determinism outside the middle class liberal groups to create a new social order; revolutionary thinking and activity is normal within it. There is a revolution of rising expectations following what mass movements have achieved in the leading countries in the area. The present world is seen as one which breeds poverty. There is in the Third World much less individualism than has been cultivated in Europe and North America, and communal forms of organization still persist.[8]

The meaning of Third World that will be used in this paper includes both Dean's development theory and Hensman's new "consciousness" concept. The Third World is made up of those people anywhere who are politically, economically, socially, educationally, or culturally oppressed: the "have-nots," the enslaved, the colonized, the oppressed, the disenfranchised.

The Third World is the world of the poor and the powerless. The first and second worlds are the worlds of the rich and the powerful. The Third World is the world of people whose needs—developmental, psychological, sociological, economic, political, and spiritual—are frustrated, thwarted, subordinated, and repressed. This is sometimes done by a statistical minority exercising majority power and dominance, as in Rhodesia, the Republic of South Africa and, to some extent, certain Latin American countries. Sometimes it is the subordination of a statistical minority by a sociological majority, as in the cases of the Black, Hispanic, Asian, and Indian-American minorities in white-dominated America. Still another instance is the subordination of a statistical minority or majority by a dominant power group from within its own population, as in the case of the masses versus the elite in Africa, Asia and Latin America, or among U.S. minorities. Finally, but by no means least, the Third World certainly includes functionally disempowered minorities such as women, homosexuals, and students.

Transcendence

Human beings are the only living creatures that possess the capacity for self-transcendence and comprehension of the phenomenon of the mysterious. Only a person can experience what Peter L. Berger refers to as an "other reality" or the "beyondness" quality of existence, the "more than" dimension of life, time, and space. Similarly, only humans have the ability to experience the mysterious, that is, to feel that what they experience is knowable but incomprehensible.

This singular, uniquely human capacity is not an independent experience. "Each individual perceives a given reality in his own characteristic way shaped by his expectations, the sum of his previous experiences, and the goal-direction of his personal intensions."[9] In other words, experiences of "otherness" derive from the matrix of the particular "existences" of the experiencing persons. These matrices occur in given periods of time and when formed into stabilized patterns or systems may be called cultural orientations. These are the milieu for personal experiencing of the transcendental and the mysterious.

Let us now trace this "transcendent" phenomenon through a four-stage developmental cycle: pretranscendentalization, transcendentalization, detranscendentalization, and retranscendentalization.

PRETRANSCENDENTALIZATION

The earliest records of human life give ample evidence of concern with both mystery and transcendence. This propensity, rooted in the capacity to think and reflect upon experience and relate it to life, was the basic survival technique of the primitive. Berger reminds us: "As cultural anthropologists have pointed out, the everyday life of primitive man was like ours, dominated by empirical, pragmatic, utilitarian imperatives geared to this world; he could hardly have solved the basic problems of survival if it had not been."[10] Primitive men accepted their world of transcendence as a matter of course. They assumed that it affected everything they did, that "the other world" impinged on this one in a variety of ways. This non-self-conscious acceptance of what Berger calls "another, supernatural world of divine beginnings and forces" is the pretranscendental period.

TRANSCENDENTALIZATION

Mircea Eliade speaks of the development of transcendental religion as an aspect of contemplation.

> Simple contemplation of the celestial vault already provokes a religious experience. The sky shows itself to be infinite, transcendent. . . . "Most high" spontaneously becomes an attribute of divinity. . . . The higher regions inaccessible to men, the sidereal zones, acquire the momentousness of the transcendent. . . . There dwell the gods.[11]

Eliade contends that with the passage of time "celestial structured supreme beings tend to disappear from the practice of religion, from cult; they depart from among men, withdraw to the sky, and become remote, inactive gods." They become the divinities of the various religions of the world religion.

In India, the earliest religious practices reflect the impact of the survival of transcendentalism. Later the Vedic hymns of the Rig Veda reflect a "numinous" quality. The Buddha, seeking to attain a higher realm of existence that would place him beyond decay, disease, and death, practiced meditative exercises, the discipline of which enabled his "enlightenment," a profoundly transcendent experience. Chinese religious thinking grew out of an animistic milieu. Though essentially oriented to the practical, it consciously or unconsciously assumes an overruling providence to which men assign themselves in moments of supreme crisis. The "crisis confidence" in the ultimate reasonableness of destiny and in the moral nature of the universe reveals both mystery and transcendence.

Mesopotamian religions (Sumerian, Babylonian, Assyrian, and Chaldean), while essentially polytheistic, worshiping nature and ancestors, had firm beliefs in sin, omens, magic, and life after death. In the religious system of the Sumerians, the basic evidence of transcendent elements can be found in the worship of An, god of Heaven. Egyptian religion in its earliest formation was a complex polytheism with three main types of gods: divinities of place, divinities of function, and cosmic divinities. There were definite traces of the transcendent elements in the cosmic god Atum, whose name means "the All."

The entire Hebrew and Christian understanding of religion is based upon a transcendent view of God. God is not an idea to be incorporated into a logical system or into a spiritual thought world, but rather is God the "totally other." The first of two main articles in the creed of Islam, "There is no God but Allah," stresses the divine nature of God. Closely related to this is Islam's emphasis on his utter transcendence: "His Throne comprises the heavens and earth. He is All-High, the All-glorious" (Koran 11, 250).

DETRANSCENDENTALIZATION AND THE THIRD WORLD

Detranscendentalization—the phenomenon that manifests a continuing disinterest in the supernatural, the mysterious, or the religious in general—is a hallmark of our generation. It has grown out of an even more comprehensive trend, secularization, the removal of large and significant areas of life from the influence of religion. Detranscendentalization and secularization, which began as early as the Renaissance and climaxed in the middle decades of the twentieth century, have been associated with and identifiable primarily in Western cultures.

For our purposes, the decline of detranscendentalism is most important. In the West, this process came full circle from transcendence to secularism, the complete and uncritical embodiment of "this worldliness." Eastern detranscendentalism presents quite a different picture. While exhibiting some "debunking" of religion per se, it has also evidenced evaluative, emergent, and functionalizing tendencies respecting transcendence and mystery. These include the resurgence of Hinduism, Buddhism, and Islam, the emergence of cults of liberation and the constructive use of religious systems as support designs for cultural identity, national integrity, and self-determination. Vittorio Lanternari expresses this in *The Religions of the Oppressed:*

> As we watch the so-called savage or backward people come to the fore and take their place on the world stage, it becomes the cultural, political, and moral duty of those who belong to a so-called cultured and elite civilization to recognize the call to freedom and liberation rising from the mouths of thousands of prophets who speak from the jungles of the Congo, from the remote islands of Melanesia, from the atolls of Polynesia, from the forgotten tribes of continental Asia, and from the Indian reservations of North America. This call, solemn and powerful because of the cultural dignity that it seeks to express, demands an answer from the Western world—and the answer must be at once political, social and religious.[12]

RESURGENCE OF THIRD WORLD RELIGIONS

A significant fact of our time is the remarkable revival of the religious traditions of the Third World nations: Hinduism, Buddhism, and Islam. The several causes for this revival need discussion before we develop the implications of transcendence and mystery implicit in some of their beliefs.

The renaissance of the Eastern religions was due at least in part to the presence of Western Christianity. First, in the missionary movement of the nineteenth century, Christianity posed a challenge to these religions. In response, they legitimated their claim to the allegiance of millions of adherents. Second, the Western Christian demonstration of power and leadership challenged the Eastern religions to respond aggressively and often defensively. Third, the achievement of political freedom on the part of Asian, African, and Latin American countries liberated indigenous religions. Finally, the revival of national culture and language lent itself to the renewal of traditional religious loyalties.

More specifically, the major Eastern religions became actively missionary. Hinduism, long a domestic and practically ethnic faith, began to seek and find converts in areas outside India. Buddhism, always missionary to some extent, began to widen the areas in which she offered the precious gift of *dharma*. Islam, which from the beginning claimed that human birth was into Islam, began to assert her mandate and seek to realize her claim outside the Near and Middle East.

These traditional religions were reasserting themselves through missions, and they were also sensing a new feeling of mission. S. Kulandran points out: "Religions that were at one time individualistic, world renouncing and world negating, now proclaim themselves to be religions designed from the outset to establish democracy and set right international chaos."[13]

TRANSCENDENCE AND BLACK AFRICA

The Third World in Africa is black Africa, that group of independent black nations, colonial black territories, and white-dominated black-majority populations struggling for liberation. In the case of the black populations in Angola, Mozambique, and Guinea-Bisau, the specific struggle is for independence or political liberation. In the case of black Africans in the Republic of South Africa (Anzania), Southwest Africa (Namibia), and Rhodesia (Zimbabwe), the specific struggle is for empowerment, especially political but also educational and economic. In the independent black nations, the struggle is against attempts to be neocolonized, and maintaining integrity and self-determination are paramount objectives. Throughout the black world in Africa, the massive general effort is to awaken in black Africans a sense of their common humanity through their "Africanness."

Three movements describe and embody this trend: Negritude, African personality, and Pan-Africanism. Negritude is a term first used by the black Martinican poet, Aime Cesaire, in 1939 in a poem, "Notebook of a Return Visit to My Native Land." Richard A. Long translates the passage as follows: " . . . Haiti where negritude rises to its feet for the first time and says that it has believed in its own humanity."[14] The original context was one of dissatisfaction on the part of West Indian students in Paris with their poetry. They were attempting to develop a content and style that would reflect their authentic African culture, rather than merely imitate the French tradition in which much of their literature had been nurtured.

The term Negritude, which has come to mean "the quality of being black" and "the notion of a consistent and historically valid nexus of black African values," was developed into a philosophical position by Leopold Sedar Senghor. "Negritude is not the defence of a skin or a colour. . . . Negritude is the awareness, defence and development of cultural values. Negritude is a myth. . . . It is the awareness by a particular group of people of its own situation in the world, and the expression of it by means of the concrete image."[15]

The African personality ideology, an aspect of the continuing struggle for new values, foundations, and identity, pertains chiefly to the arts. E. Mphahlele, in *The African Image*, states his belief that the African artist who works with "African themes, rhythms and idiom . . . cannot but express an African personality. There need be no mystique about it."[16] Mphahlele also warns that the African must not use art exclusively as a polemic for African nationalism. "But if he thinks of the African Personality as a battle cry, it's bound to throw him into a stance, an attitude, and his art will suffer."[17] Rather would Mphahlele have the African artist become authentic as an artist: "Every artist in the world, African or not, must go through the agony of purging his art of imitations and false notes before he strikes an individual medium. Leave the artist to this evolution: let him sweat it out and be emancipated by his own art."[18] A wider definition of African personality is offered by Alioun Diop:

> The African personality, which is the basis and foundation of our humanism, aspires . . . to being freed from the Western grip. It requires that our people should speak through us. . . . Our people only mean to give expression to what they alone can show forth: how they can see themselves, how they identify themselves in the context of the world situation and of the great problems of mankind.[19]

Pan-Africanism began in 1900 with the First Pan-African Congress, held in London as a movement to unify persons of African descent across the world. Following World War I the Congress made a futile attempt to obtain self-determination for black African countries and populations. After World War II its leadership and program shifted to black Africa, where it became the instrument of African nationalism, climaxing in the formation of the Organization of African Unity (OAU) in Addis Ababa in 1963.

The genius of Pan-Africanism is best described, in the words of A. A. Maxrui, as the principle of "African oneness," opposed to colonization, factionalism, tribalism, and class distinctions. Taken as a whole it is what Mazrui calls a "mystique of a classless Africa."[20]

Negritude, African personality, and Pan-Africanism are illustrations of catalytic movements stimulating black Africans to transcend themselves, reject the stereotypes imputed by the first and second worlds and thus position themselves to make their full contribution as persons to the life and work of the human community. Three elements in this stance of the "new" black African are particularly relevant to a discussion of transcendence and mystery. In the concept of Negritude, the African comes to a new sense of awareness of his full humanity from within the context of his African history and culture. He transcends the old myths and embraces a new identity, "beyond" him but nonetheless real for him. The African personality ideology is a rhetorical exhortation to articulate one's Africanness, but only as a vehicle for one's responsibility to be human in the universal sense. Pan-Africanism represents the transcendent tendency at work as it symbolizes an ideal toward which to strive (African oneness), despite the low probability of attainment.

Perhaps the principle Richardson and Cutler suggest about primitive mankind can apply to all mankind of any period in history: "Anthropologists generally agree that in situations of life crisis and emotional stress primitive man experienced rescue through myths that showed him a way of escape where empirically none had existed."[21]

In Negritude, African personality, and Pan-Africanism, there are mythic elements. Yet who is to say that they are not relevant or meaningful? Here one is inclined to agree with Harvey Cox, who in discussing how religion contributes to a society's capacity of social transcendence, says that "it does so by symbolizing an ideal toward which to strive and by doing so with sufficient affective power that the ideal provides a real source of motivation."[22]

TRANSCENDENCE AND LATIN AMERICA

Many observers have described the current Latin American Revolution as basically a "struggle for humanization." This will be the second Third World model to be examined, to demonstrate the capacity for "socio-cultural transcendence or the gift for imagining radically alternative futures."[23]

The transcendent dimensions of the Latin American revolutionary situation are hope and revolution. Both are undergirded by a long-term program of "conscientization" of the masses. In the work of Paulo Freire, a Brazilian, this essentially Christian humanist philosophy concerns itself with radical humanization. Freire's basic question is How can the depressed and oppressed masses in Latin America move toward full human existence as persons? He believes it is possible only if the masses can be liberated from social, governmental, and possibly even religious structures and view themselves anew as participating persons in a concrete historical process that is open to the future.

In other words, the capacity for both human and social transcendence has been articulated and focused on whatever obstructs millions of nations (sic) in Latin America not only from fulfilling themselves but from realizing that they are unfulfilled. Under the leadership of such men as Paulo Freire and Rubem Alves, the "consciousness of oppression" is being raised. Essentially this means that the Third World Latin American's view of himself, his condition, his fellowmen, his history, and his destiny are being critically reviewed.

This process is being accomplished through radical dialogue. Groups of people are assembled in dialogue about their humanity. In the words of J. DaViega Coutinho: "To discover their own humanity, to realize they are subjects in the transformation of their own lives, of their own countries. It is not so much what they have but what they think of themselves that is decisive."[24]

Another aspect of discovering humanity is language. South Americans, especially, are being taught the language of consciousness expression, or language as the shared expression and definition of experience. Through this language, men speak honestly and urgently about the common experience of oppression they share. They speak about the repressive measures used against them in their countries in the place of justice. They speak about the failure of reform programs that cannot succeed because of the unaltered political, economic, and educational structures. South Americans are further sensitized in this new language to the cooperation of the churches in the oppression of the poor because of their preoccupation with pietistic standards and personal salvation, often oblivious to the social, economic, and political realities that face the masses. Great emphasis is placed on the general bankruptcy of the educational systems of the South American continent, which do little more than mimic the lifestyles of the elite, support the status quo, and sidestep basic social changes.

Rubem Alves, in A *Theology of Human Hope*, continues and explains the fuller implications of language as a key to consciousness. It can be and is a two-edged sword. On the one hand, it creates a new community of understanding, while on the other, it creates a community of "incomprehension." Even as it delineates the situation of the oppressed it juxtaposes their situation to that of the oppressor.

The example he uses is that of the rise of technology. It is also a language, just as much as the language of the consciousness of oppression. The language of technology assumes that all society's problems can be solved by a greater technology. But once such a statement is made, language becomes more than speech. It becomes a program. Further, it becomes a program that in the very process of feeding people dehumanizes them, and in the process of educating them narcotizes their humanity.

Yet the language of technology is a way of life, which has been predetermined as good for the development of "underdeveloped" or "developing" nations, and therefore it is in direct opposition to the language of the consciousness of oppression. This language is saying that technological man is "futureless." At best it can accomplish some quantitative change. What is needed is qualitative change, the kind of change that will liberate instead of domesticate.

Conscientization demonstrates the capacity for self-transcendence and sociocultural transcendence most clearly in its interpretation of God's relation to history and the future. According to Alves, God is both historical and futuristic. His presence in history is the presence of the future and since his presence in history is always resisted, God becomes (or is) a suffering God.[25] God, then, becomes the suffering "slave." This capacity of God transcendent to suffer is the ground of hope for our liberation. For in suffering with him, the oppressed will be victorious even as God has been, is, and will be victorious.

Alves goes on to say that there is another way God suffers. He suffers when the oppressed become and remain domesticated—when man is no longer his companion in the politics of freedom. This, then, is the rationale for revolution—that the oppressed join the God of the future, present in liberating struggles for mankind.

RETRANSCENDENTALIZATION

Retranscendentalization, the renewal of the importance of the supernatural or the "other" quality of human thought and religion, has several manifestations in the Third World. The prophetic secular and religious movements for liberation among people who are ethnologically at early levels of development are examples. "Probably there is no phenomenon which reflects more clearly than do the religious movements among oppressed people, the contradictory, yet indissoluble bond between current reality and future goals, between history and eschatology, which lies at the root of almost every major human experience."[26]

Transcendence and mystery, the unexplainable and "otherness" aspects of human experience, are human universals. Secular or religious movements that lie at the base of social and political activity in the Third World are rooted in or grow out of transcendental motivations or experiences. As Berger states: "In the religious view of reality, all phenomena point toward that which transcends them, and this transcendence actively impinges from all sides on the empirical sphere of human existence."[27]

We have seen that the transcendent experience has had high functional and utility value among the oppressed in terms of symbol, strategy, and strength. Huston Smith points out that "what we can say more confidently is that the guise in which transcendence appears varies with the mode of life deficiency. Those who suffer from bondage and confinement see it as promising liberation and expansion."[28]

It is reasonable to conclude that the transcendent and the mysterious have affected and will continue to affect, in various and significant ways, the perspective on and treatment of the issues and problems of liberation, development, and nation building in countries of the Third World. Finally, the unique contribution of certain emphases and developments in non-Western views of mystery and transcendence can enable first and second world people to reevaluate their understanding of the individual, in terms of ampler meanings of personhood. Berger says:

> A rediscovery of the supernatural will be, above all, a regaining of openness in our perception of reality. . . . In openness to the signals of transcendence the true proportions of our experience are rediscovered. . . . [This has] a moral significance, even a political significance . . . it permits a confrontation with the age in which one lives in a perspective that transcends the age and thus puts it in proportion.[29]

What word does all this say to the Christian? It tells us that we cannot despair at the world situation today or view as inevitable the worsening of its problems of poverty and oppression. Marshall McLuhan's words must be taken seriously: "There is absolutely no inevitability as long as there is a willingness to contemplate what is happening." Transcendence and mystery, the unknowable and the beyond, are experiences in which God himself waits to join us in the human struggle for liberation.

Liberation Theology, Black Theology, and Religious Education

In an early essay, Shockley articulates the rationale that guided his quest for a new way of thinking about religious education for the rest of his active career—a way of thinking that takes seriously the possibilities in liberation and black theologies for a liberative education in the black church. It includes page 80 and following in *Foundations for Christian Education in an Era of Change* (Nashville: Abingdon, 1976) with Marvin J. Taylor as editor.

"Of the Dawn of Freedom" entitles chapter 2 of *The Souls of Black Folk* by the brilliant black American scholar, W. E. B. DuBois. In the opening sentences of that chapter are his words, "The problem of the twentieth century is the problem of the color line,—the relation of the darker to the lighter races of men in Asia and Africa, in America and the islands of the sea." Fifty years later (1953), DuBois republished this book. When asked if he still affirmed his position he responded:

> I still think today as yesterday that the color line is a great problem of this century. But today I see more clearly than yesterday that back of the problem of race and color lies a greater problem which both obscures and implements it: and that is the fact that so many civilized persons are willing to live in comfort even if the price of this is poverty, ignorance and disease of the majority of their fellowmen.[30]

This addendum brings into sharp focus three issues that will be discussed in this chapter: human oppression in its various dehumanizing forms; liberation programs and their signs of hope; and religious education, potentially an enabling means toward the end of realizing "love, power, and justice" for all persons. These issues, which constitute a challenge to the churches, are restated by Lerone Bennett, Jr., historian of the black revolution in America, and Paulo Freire, liberationist educator of Latin America. Bennett said: "We can see that challenge in its clearest form in the educational field. . . . For blackness raises total questions about the meaning of education in a situation of oppression . . . an educator in a situation of oppression is either an oppressor or a liberator." Brazilian educator Freire at the Bergen World Consultation on Education held in Holland said: "There is no such thing as neutral education. Education is either for liberation or against liberation and therefore in favor of domination."[31]

The challenge to the education programs of churches in these statements is clear, and it raises several insistent questions for the religious educator. Rosemary R. Ruether articulates some of these from the life of a local congregation:

> What kind of Christian education is possible in America in the third quarter of the twentieth century . . . where our cultural forms and institutions taken for granted have become quaint cultural artifacts and where the name "Christian" seems a more and more parochial image. What kind of Christian Education is possible in a world of youth and revolution, black revolution, and world challenge to imperialism?[32]

In attempting to resolve these questions, Euro-American theology has not been too helpful and has often been reluctant, if not reactionary. Some of the reasons for this necessitate the brief historical background that follows.

During the nineteenth century, Calvinism and revivalism united to form a "New England" system of theology, emphasizing repentance, conversion, and personal piety. With the passing of the western frontier, the advent of Darwinism, the historical-critical method of biblical study, urbanization, and strong criticisms of Calvinism, New England orthodoxy gave way to "Evangelical Liberalism," putting stress on freedom, growth, choice, and progress. Its most notable achievement was the initiation of the Social Gospel Movement (1876–1917). Between 1919 and 1939, Karl Barth's influence and insistence upon "desecularizing" the gospel by getting rid of all "entangling alliances" with science and philosophy dominated the theological scene. Important for this chapter is the fact that Barth's anti-empirical posture militated against movement that could have enriched American religion's understanding of the then future phenomenon of the Third World and the already desperate racial issue in America. Actually, theological investigation during this period (1900–40), excepting the critiques of H. Richard Niebuhr (1929) and Reinhold Niebuhr (1932), almost totally neglected the black experience.[33] Similarly, Euro-American theology neglected contact with the rapidly growing fields of the social sciences, especially education. In religious education theory development, curriculum construction, and teaching systems were moving in the direction of social concerns and criticism. Excepting the work of George A. Coe, however, even religious educators paid scant attention to racism. The Sunday school movement found the black population a source of continual embarrassment to the churches, despite their aim to carry it to "every destitute place."[34] Horace Bushnell, considered the founder of modern Protestant religious education in America, was a firm believer in the racist doctrine of Manifest Destiny and its corollary, white (specifically Anglo-Saxon) superiority. To Bushnell, Indians were "among the feebler, wilder races" and, together with black people, were only salvable through assimilation. Bushnell, however, did desire slaveholders to acknowledge "the immortal mind and manhood of your slave," but he also believed "that the African race in this country, would soon begin to dwindle towards extinction . . . if emancipated."[35]

Not until the publication of Coe's *What Is Religion Doing to Our Consciences?* (1943) did religious educators in America begin to examine, even generally, this critical dimension of responsibility. In 1965 Randolph C. Miller (Bushnell Professor at Yale) wrote in relation to the involvement of religious education in the social sphere that it was "one of the untravelled roads in contemporary Christian thinking." In the same paper, he also felt obliged to say, "slowly the churches have become aware of the Christian interpretation of race relations. . . . To some extent, the recognition of this problem is finding its way into Christian education."[36]

In the theological arena in America, parties in the church-society dichotomy began to show signs of desiring unification and serious dialogue after World War II. As a result of the landmark meeting of Euro-American theologians at the Cambridge (England) Conference on International Affairs (1945), theological trends began to move "toward constructive rather than polemical thinking." During the fifties and the sixties the center of gravity in Euro-American theological thought moved rather boldly from a past-oriented traditional stance to a present-oriented, if not an existentialist, posture. Included in this reorientation were the emergence of such movements as the "new hermeneutic," attempting to interpret more authentically the biblical past in the present; "secular theology" and its efforts to draw theology "increasingly into a new worldliness" with freedom to fashion the future; and "theologies of hope," engaging the world and Christians in future-oriented history-making in the "now" of the present.

A question is posed by this historical survey of the response (or rather the lack of it) of theology and religious education to the insistent cry of "the wretched of the earth" for liberation and development.[37] Why, except for its racism (and elitism), has religious education in America failed to see its responsibility for applying its recent research and insights about change and humanization to the poor and minorities? This inability or unwillingness or both posed the dilemma that both "liberation theology" and "black theology" sought to resolve.

Christian Education and the Black Church

This next contribution from the writings of Grant Shockley is the introduction to a lecture he gave to a conference on Christian education in the black church in 1985. In this lecture Shockley expanded and refined his discussion of the history of the black experience with religious education in the previous section of this book. In the introduction to the lecture however, he introduces a new theme into his writing. The religious education experience of black Christians was the source for the black church's contribution to the larger discussion of religious education. In the process he claimed a mutuality for black and white in programmatic and constructive thinking about religious education. The lecture was published in Charles R. Foster, Ethel R. Johnson, and Grant S. Shockley, *Christian Education Journey of Black Americans: Past, Present, Future* (Nashville: Discipleship Resources, 1985): 1-2.

This essay reflects a metamorphosis in my own thinking over the past thirty-five years of involvement in various aspects of the church's educational ministry. I have struggled with the issues that provide the focus of this essay as a local church pastor, a seminary professor, a member of the Curriculum Resources Committee, and a member of the Board of Discipleship.[38] Emerging from that struggle in recent years, several assumptions have increasingly informed my understanding of Christian education in the black church.

1. Throughout the history of Christian education, the black experience has changed Christian education in the American church, and Christian education has also shaped the black experience. This interplay has significantly influenced all our lives, even though the details of the story have been, for the most part, hidden from our view.

2. I am assuming that my black readers conceive of themselves as black. Our blackness is unchangeable. It is with us and we are with it for all our future. The recognition of this fact is crucial if we are to recognize and acknowledge the basic "over-againstness" of black and white in our society. Each is here to stay. We cannot run from each other. We cannot make believe the other does not exist. We cannot gloss over or redefine each other. We have to deal with each other in the context of what this means for the church, its missions, and its ministries.

At the same time, it is futile to project a future involving separatism of any kind. If the church has done anything, it should have conveyed to us that through the grace of God in Christ, we are able to relate to our blackness in a positive way. And we are able to relate to the whiteness that surrounds our blackness in a graceful and constructive way, with the realization that neither of us can change. Hence we approach this discussion of Christian education out of the context of our common black experience.

3. We must be committed to Christian education from the standpoint of the black experience. But I am making an important distinction. There is no such thing as black Christian education. Our view of Christian education has been shaped by our experience and that experience has been black. Our commitment to Christian education embodies both a theory and a practice grounded in that experience. This commitment cannot be a general one. It has to be a commitment to a program that actively enacts the incarnation in the midst of the distinctive realities of the world which mark black and white relationships in this country.

4. I am assuming we all have faith in the future, which will bring us into the sunlight of the kingdom of God—a world over which God rules and reigns among all people and in whom we may discern our unity. That is where we are headed, but we are not there yet. So we must be guided by an interim ethic, an interim practice, an interim program. To accept the challenge of the future toward which we move, we must know our past as well—not the past as it has so often been told us, but the past as we have experienced it. And that task is the one that lies before us.

5. Christian educators in the black church are beginning to recognize some new issues involved in defining their task. Primary among these questions are not only the standard ones regarding objectives, content, curriculum, learning, teaching, leadership, and evaluation, but also the more insistent and crucial questions of the relationship of these areas of concern to the black experience, the black community, the black church,

black theology, and black liberation. The questions concerning this relationship emerged in the ferment of the 1960s Civil Rights Movement and continue to this day relatively unchanged.

As they are viewed by the black church, these questions are essentially contextual. From goal-setting to evaluating, black educators in black churches are viewing the educational process in relation to the kind of learning and teaching that considers the black experience as central and the liberation of black people as its focal point. From this perspective Christian education may be defined as that process which teaches concepts, attitudes, and skills that facilitate meaningful learning in relation to the black experience and the church's implicit task of humanization and liberation.

Black Theology and Religious Education

This excerpt is drawn from an essay entitled "Black Theology and Religious Education" published in Randolph Crump Miller, ed., *Theologies of Religious Education* (Birmingham: Religious Education Press, 1995), pages 314-21. As one of his last published essays it reveals the maturing of his thinking about a Christian education grounded in the black religious experience. It also illustrates something of the style of his scholarly work in its recapitulation, expansion, and refinement of themes from his earliest writings. We have included the last section of this essay that focuses Shockley's quest for a model of religious education on its sources in Black Theology. In this decision Shockley continued to use the theory to practice approach to model building that is deeply rooted in the intellectual traditions of Western Europe.

Introduction

The objectives of this chapter on black theology and religious education are two: (1) to explore the background and current situation in black theology and (2) to discuss the impact and implications of black theology for the theory and practice of religious education primarily in black churches. The background and content section will discuss: the origins of black theology; reactions to black theology; definition and sources of black theology; black theologies and theologians; and an assessment of black theology.

Origins of Black Theology

Black theology has been aptly referred to as the most fruitful and exciting theological development in North America. It had its inception with the publication of the Black Power Statement by the National Committee of Negro Churchmen in 1966. This statement had come as the result of a decision of a group of black clergy to endorse the then-emerging Black Power movement. The argument of the statement was a deep concern that the "important human realities" in the controversy about black power not be ignored because of militant rhetoric and strident language. "The fundamental distortion facing us on the controversy of black power," they said, "is rooted in a gross imbalance of power and conscience between Negro and White Americans."[39] Further, these clergy made it clear that they would no longer abide by the assumption

> That white people are justified in getting what they want through the use of power, but that Negro Americans must, either by nature or by circumstances, make their appeal only through conscience. As a result. . . . the power of white men is corrupted because it meets little resistance. . . . The conscience of black men is corrupted because, having no power to implement the demands of conscience, the concern for justice is transmuted into a distorted form of love, which in the absence of justice, becomes chaotic self-surrender. Powerlessness creates a race of beggars. We are faced now with a situation where conscience-less power meets powerless conscience, threatening the very foundations of our nation.[40]

Much of the tumult surrounding black theology centered around this early association with Black Power and the continued insistence "that black people must have the capacity to participate with power, i.e., organized political and economic strength to really influence people with whom . . . [they] . . . interact."

A second major goal of the black theology movement was the eradication of racism in the general society as well as in white church structures. Defined by the Uppsala Assembly of the World Council of Churches in 1968 as "ethnocentric pride" with the "thrust to discriminate against and exclude,"[41] this social cancer has wrought havoc with the lives and hopes of the rejected and powerless for centuries.

Under the guise of "Manifest Destiny" it has condoned and allowed white settlers in America to confiscate from the Indians most of the land which now comprises the United States.[42] Racism contributed to the corruption of the social, economic, and political structure of the nation (North and South) through the system of chattel slave labor, "the vilest that ever saw the sun."[43] Spanish American lands were taken in illegal wars of "territorial expansion," and Asian Americans, whose poorly paid labor developed much of the west and its farmlands, were "rewarded" with racist-inspired exclusion acts and relocation (detention camps) centers.[44]

The classic and most dramatic example of racism in America was its black population who, since the early seventeenth century, had endured in both the churches and the general society every conceivable form of abuse. They were considered only three-fifths human in the Constitution of "the most enlightened democracy on earth." In 1854 the Supreme Court maintained that black people "had no rights that whites were bound to respect." In 1896 the Supreme Court legalized the segregation of its "free" citizens on the basis of skin color. The United Nations was not three years old (1947) when it received from the black constituency of the United States, a charter member, a document entitled "A Statement on the Denial of Human Rights to Minorities in the Case of Citizens of Negro descent in the United States of America and an Appeal for Redress." It was 1954 before the Supreme Court recognized that the 1896 decision was a travesty upon justice and that separate in an open society is by definition "unequal." In 1964 and 1965 Congress legislated its first comprehensive civil rights bills in a century, including the right of franchise for millions of disfranchised black people in the South. The years 1964–66 were years of disenchantment. The Civil Rights movement crested with Martin Luther King's eloquent "I Have a Dream" address (Washington, D.C., 1963). In 1964–65 deep frustration developed as unenforceable laws were substituted for justice and tokenism in employment for comprehensive fair-employment practices.

Succinctly, by the late 1960s the extremity of most black patience, with gradualism, legalism, tinkering reform, and conciliation was reached. Then it came—the black revolution for power—Black Power! This movement galvanized the white (and some sectors of the black) community. It was a totally new, "audacious" way for black people to act. It meant a new assessment of power—not only to achieve equality of opportunity but to achieve equality of advantage and results. With this new concept of power other insights were born. Black power came to signify a new understanding of one's blackness, worth, dignity, and heritage. It meant affirmation rather than negation, activity rather than passivity, self-pride instead of self-hate. In this new light, black survival meant black control. Educational, economic, social, political, and religious institutions must become imbued with black self-determination.

Reactions to Black Theology

Generally, what had been the witness of the churches in the long struggle for black civil rights and liberation from white racism? At best it had been paternalistic. But in terms of the mandate of the gospel it had been (and still is) reluctant. It had acquiesced in segregation, failed to identify, define, or articulate critically or challenge effectively a single aspect of the problem of racism faced by almost 15 percent of its national population, 80 percent of whom were fellow Christians.

While the churches did produce, periodically, sincere dissenting voices who exerted a positive though not a crucial influence, it is only honest to say that this was the limit of their participation. Further, as the black revolution escalated in the direction of challenging the root systems of power that enabled racism and called to accountability the centers of power that supported it, most, though not all, of the white "liberal" voices receded into the background. At this point, two things became clear. The black struggle for justice and liberation must become independent. There could be no sure reliance on white "reformers." The struggle would have to seek a base of support within the black community and most likely in the black churches. Second, the black churches themselves would have to be committed to the black masses and their liberation. A new generation of black youth began to question the credentials of an institution that could not or would not act courageously on issues it claimed were aborting its mission, violating its fellowship, and mocking its witness. It was this situation in the general society and in the church which gave birth to a liberation movement of its own, one that would combine the yet remaining faith of black people in the black church and their new determination to obtain corrective justice.

Definitions and Sources of Black Theology

Black theology became the name of the movement that "religiocified" Black Power. It was a unique and indigenous development on the American theological scene. More than a "blackenized" version of Euro-

American theology, it was a new way of "doing" theology. Its mission was to raise new questions, develop novel concepts, and pattern new motifs about the basic nature of the Christian faith in relation to the black experience, forcing a reconsideration "if not a redefinition of every major theological category." James Cone states the matter very clearly in an early definition: "What is Black Theology? Black Theology is that theology which arises out of the need to articulate the significance of Black presence in a hostile white world. It is Black people reflecting religiously on the Black experience, attempting to redefine the relevance of the Christian Gospel for their lives."[45]

Originating in the midst of the black struggle for liberation, black theology not only developed a unique objective and definition but a novel set of sources as well. These are identifiable as the following: (1) the Civil Rights movement; (2) Joseph Washington's *Black Religion* (1964); (3) the Black Revolution (1966); and (4) the dialogue among theologians outside the United States.

The Civil Rights struggle for equality was a primary source for developing a black theology. Its data began with fierce resistance to enslavement, slave rebellions, Underground Railroad escapes, and Civil War participation. In this century every known form of protest including litigation at every judicial level was explored. Since 1950 there have been additional strategic expressions in the liberation struggle. The first of these was the Freedom Movement (1955–65). This brought the politicization of the black masses and the rise of a strong black leadership class personified in the brilliant leadership of Martin Luther King Jr. (1929–68).

The publication of *Black Religion* by Joseph Washington[46] ushered in another critical period in the black struggle for liberation. Often referred to as "one of the most important works in the history of black theology" it was a pivotal source for later black religion and theology protest writers such as Vincent Harding, Charles Long, and especially James Cone. A brief summary of the contents of Washington's *Black Religion* illustrates its importance as a point of departure for Cone, Long, and others. Washington makes several assertions: (1) Black people are not a part of the "mainstream" Christian tradition in theology; (2) nor do they have "authentic" roots in the historical Christian tradition; (3) they seem to lack an ecumenical vision; and (4) for all practical purposes they do not exclude non-blacks but neither do they seem to intentionally include them. Agreement or disagreement with Washington's allegations aside, his work made a necessary critique of the nascent black theology movement. It did this by raising fundamental questions about the nature, purpose, and forms of black religion. These questions initiated a dialogue which preoccupied black theology for at least two decades.

Not long after Washington's *Black Religion* created its sensational stir, the Black Revolution enveloped the black community. Much of the 1966–76 decade witnessed the escalation of essentially nonviolent but confrontational strategies in the achievement of black liberation goals. A new and fiercely independent black leadership cadre spoke of "black identity," "black self-determination," and "black power." Interracial dialogues were often replaced by painful periods of "strategic disengagement" with whites. Black church "caucuses" were initiated. Black heritage reclamation and black cultural indigenization became normative. Politicization had become radicalization. Needless to say this traumatic period provided the definitive input for the then emerging black theology paradigm.[47]

A fourth source that influenced the development of black theology was the many dialogues with theologians outside the United States. Teaching exchanges, conferences, and publications between African, European, Asian, Latin American, and North American theologians and black theologians (since about 1976) served to broaden and deepen the study of black theology.[48]

The fifth and most recent source of influence in the development of black theology has been the growing conversation with black women. The recent publication of Jacqueline Grant's influential essay, "White Woman's Christ and Black Woman's Jesus: Feminine Christology and Womanist Response," has done much to visualize and critique black male predominance in the theological arena. More than that, however, it has called into question several assumptions about women in liberation theology and especially black theology.[49]

Black Theologies and Theologians

The Civil Rights Movement, anti-civil rights intransigence, sexism, and white church reluctance to move beyond rhetoric and the safe confines of pious liberal pronouncements to basic reform, forced black people to reconsider, redefine, and reconstruct their worldview and religious faith. The result of this new mood in the secular sphere was the cry for Black Power. In the religious domain it was black theology.

James Cone, in his pivotal volume *Black Theology and Black Power*, outlined the direction of this new departure in American theological thought, the first ever to challenge its dominance from a social perspective.[50] He made several definitive assertions: (1) theology can be done independently of any previous paradigm, and it can be done from a black perspective; (2) black theology is and ought to be a theology of and for the oppressed; (3) black theology originated in the struggle of the black church on behalf of the black masses; (4) black theology is a valid explication of the role that God has always played in the history of his people.

Cone's "theology of black power" for black liberation became the major voice in the Black Theology Movement. There were and are other positions, however. Albert Cleage in his *Black Messiah* (1968) provided a thoroughly black nationalist interpretation of both black religion and the black church. J. Deotis Roberts in his *Liberation and Reconciliation: A Black Theology* (1971), while not denying the importance of liberation insists that it must be preceded by reconciliation. Major Jones theologizing from a "theology of hope" position in his *Black Awareness: A Theology of Hope* (1971), believes that black theology is valid as it moves the black church toward the new community beyond racism of any kind. Charles Long in key articles (1971 and 1975) questions the very legitimacy of black theology if based on Western rather than African theological thought. Gayraud Wilmore, basically agreeing with Long but still adhering to James Cone's black theology tradition, contends in his *Black Religion and Black Radicalism* (1972) that black radicalism can best be validated in a black theology based on black religion rather than on a "black version of white theology based on Black Power." Cecil Cone, the brother of James Cone, adds a significant statement to the black theology discussion with his position that black theology grows out of African Christian, black religious, and black church roots.[51] Yet another voice is heard on the black theology issue. William Jones in *Is God a White Racist?* (1973) introduces the problem of suffering into the black theology discussion. He holds the position, from a black humanistic perspective, that black theology is an anomaly since it cannot be empirically demonstrated that God either exists or has ever really delivered black people from oppression.

An Assessment of Black Theology

The prior brief look at the background, growth, and development of black theology leads naturally to an assessment of its value, worth, and relevance to the black church and to religious education. It has done several things. *First,* it has challenged the black church to engage itself effectively in the liberation of oppressed black people. This challenge has historic significance. It marks the first time in the history of church life in America that a radical minority group or movement has aggressively challenged the theological assumptions of the Christian faith on the basis of its own ethic of inclusiveness and justice. Also it is the first time that a color-minority has articulated such a protest in the form of a radically alternative system and church style, that is, black theology and a public program of social liberation.

Second, black theology has caused the black church to see religious education from an entirely new perspective. Black theology suggests that there is now "a felt need to reconstruct a worldview as it concerns an entire people."[52] That worldview illuminates a new future that black people can have. It is a future in which they believe and know that they can be free if they want that freedom enough to suffer, sacrifice, and perhaps even die for it.

Third, black theology teaches black people that they must develop and initiate a black agenda. Liberation begins with "me" and with "us." It is not something that can be done for us. In solidarity with others in similar situations of oppression—women, Asians, Latinos, Native Americans—"consciousness" must be raised, identity must be self-affirmed and liberation—our liberation—must be claimed.

Fourth, black theology has confronted black people with the realization that religious education in our context must include transformation as well as information. Religious education fulfills a highly normative function when it seeks to guide the teaching/learning process to the end that justice and a new humanity may emerge.

Finally, black theology has been instructive at the point of letting us know that any religious education program that might be constructed must grow out of and center around the experiences, relationships, and situational dilemmas that black people face in their day-to-day struggle to survive, develop, and progress in an often hostile, uncaring, majority-dominated society. A corollary to this is a continuous and faithful search for practices, methods, and techniques that embody, complement, and reinforce this principle.

SECTION III

The Quest for a Model

Introduction

Foster: Although Grant spent most of his career in the academy, his attention never wandered far from the needs of congregations. He led workshops in congregations, preached regularly in congregations, taught about congregations, and concluded most of his essays with an exploration of implications for the educational ministry of congregations. He believed that the quality and character of congregational ministry depended upon the quality and character of its education. And when he looked at the church in general and the black church in particular, he was dismayed by what he saw.

Smith: He described his quest for a more adequate education as the quest for a model for the church's education. From his earliest writings on the subject in the 1970s the sources for this model were clear: Black Theology, liberation pedagogy, and the life and experience of the black church, especially in the city. In essay after essay he would return to these themes, expanding and refining his earlier discussion with insights from his latest reading and from his most recent conversations with church and academic leaders.

Foster: His quest for a model occurred at a time when many leaders in education were convinced that they could develop a cognitive map for structuring an education in churches, communities, even nations that drew on their deepest and most cherished values and extended them into the lives of subsequent generations. It was an optimistic task—one filled with great hope, a theme that permeates Shockley's writings on the future of Christian education explicitly for the black church but also through the black church for the church in general.

Smith: In a seminary class on "Christian Education in the Black Religious Experience," in which I was using several of Shockley's essays, a student articulated Shockley's hope as clearly as anyone. He observed that jazz originated in the black experience, was intended originally for a black audience, but touched a nerve in the experience of peoples from many diverse cultural and national backgrounds and influenced music much more widely. In a similar way, the depth of the pathos in the black religious experience also has a surplus of meaning so to speak, so that its possibilities exceed the actual experience of those for whom it is intended. Grant spent his life trying to systematize that experience so that it could be a wellspring for the life of faith in the black church and a resource for the education of all Christians. In that effort we can see a clear trajectory of thinking toward an understanding of Christian religious education originating in the black religious experience with relevance to the religious education of all Christians.

Foster: In a sense however, he never fully succeeded in that task. When he began working on this task he lacked indigenous resources into the Black religious experience. The basic ignorance of his white audiences of the most basic information about the black experience in general and the religious experience of African Americans in particular presented him with a persistent challenge. He could rarely assume a residue of common experience and knowledge in the development of his ideas. This meant that in every lecture he gave, paper he wrote, or course he taught, he felt the imperative to introduce his audience to basic themes in the black experience. The academy moreover did not recognize for a long time the legitimacy of scholarship focused on and shaped by the social, cultural, economic, political, and religious dynamics in the daily lives of African Americans. There, too, he encountered an ignorance of the issues, concerns, and experience that dominated his thinking. He had to address that ignorance in ways that could be heard.

Smith: It is at this point that we again see the influence of his own double consciousness on his thinking. As one who mediated the theological worlds of black and white in church and seminary contexts, he celebrated his black heritage and drew on the resources of that heritage and experience, while always conscious of its perception and reception by his white audiences. This called for a distinctive imaginative capacity not required of scholars writing for culturally and racially specific constituencies. It is an imagination grounded in the capacity for resistance against domination, survival from oppression, and resilience in the midst of overwhelming ambiguity. The primary resources for that imaginative capacity he found in the conversations on Black Theology. Even as he discerned significant educational implications in the constructive work of those conversations, however, he was apparently unaware that in the effort to develop an educational model from Black Theology he was still working out of an intellectual framework of theory to practice contrary both to the epistemological assumptions in the Freirian pedagogy he espoused and the African heritage he honored. As the heirs to his work it is not easy for us to appreciate the difficulty to be found in this effort. It calls not only for a recasting of ideas but a transformation of perceptions and habits integral to the work of scholarship.

Foster: Shockley could have left his mark on the life of the church and academy simply as an interpreter and mediator of the black religious experience for his black and white audiences. But he was not satisfied with that task. His attention from his earliest writing was directed to the constructive task of developing a model of Christian education for the black church that would, at the same time, illumine and influence conversations in the church and academic worlds on the religious education of all Christians. It is in this effort that the struggle of his imagination to break through the bondage of double consciousness to the giftedness of double consciousness becomes most evident.

Smith: He took on this constructive task in most of his writings on Christian education. We had to make several decisions, therefore, about what from all he wrote about a model of Christian education for the black church we could include in this volume. We could have chosen selections to illustrate the gradual evolution of his thinking about Black Theology and liberation pedagogy in religious education. We could also have contrasted early and later versions of the model he worked on throughout his career. We chose neither of these options. Instead we decided to focus attention on his response to the conversations that most challenged his thinking about the future shape of religious education.

Foster: We have highlighted three of these conversations. The first we have already introduced in earlier sections of this volume. It occurred at the confluence of three centers of intellectual ferment—around the themes and methods of Black Theology, Liberation Theology, and liberative pedagogy. In the first essay that follows, Shockley gathers up the dominant themes from his engagement with these three intellectual movements. In the "New Black Church Challenge to Religious Education" that follows, Shockley draws on that conversation to articulate a shift in the focus of his thinking about religious education. From this point forward his attention is on the development of a model that reflects the vision and mission of what he calls "the new Black church"—that church grounded in and shaped by Black Theology as informed by the insights of liberation theology and liberative pedagogy. In this essay he begins to call his vision for that education an "intentional-engagement model" to reflect the political as well as missional character of the convergence of these themes in his thinking. From this point forward a black religious education functions in his mind as a partner in the conversations on the future of religious education and not as a recipient of those conversations.

Smith: Even as Shockley was developing increasing clarity about the partnership of black with white religious education, the larger conversations in education were responding to the pressures of an increasing range of cultural and ethnic perspectives on the education of the church and of the nation. These conversations on what soon was to be called "multicultural education" reflected the power dynamics at work among the various cultural and racial groups of the nation. Perhaps most insidious in predominantly white denominations was the designation of all other racial and cultural groups as "ethnic minorities." In the third essay in this section Shockley takes on the challenge of sorting through what it means for African Americans (and by implication the rest of us as well) to be "ethnic" in any consideration of the church's education.

Foster: Another issue that began to catch the attention of religious educators in the 1980s emerged from the increasing encounters of Christians with adherents of the other great world religions. This was not a new issue for Shockley. He had witnessed Christians, in Africa and Asia in particular, working out their own educational missions in the midst of religiously diverse societies—indeed often as minorities in those societies. This encounter, however, raised for Shockley the question about how to think through the relationship of cultural to religious pluralism in the development of a model for the future of Christian education in the black church. That is the subject of the fourth selection of his writing to be found in this section.

Smith: In the fifth selection Shockley articulates the primary characteristics of an "intentional-engagement model" for religious education. It sets the stage for the last section of this chapter—his last major essay on Christian religious education written in 1995. In it Shockley draws together many of the themes that he had been working on for the previous twenty years. It set the stage for the book that he hoped to write on Christian education in the black religious experience.

The Confluence of Black and Liberation Theologies and Liberative Pedagogies

The following discussion of "Black Theology and Christian Education" is the concluding section of a paper entitled "Christian Education and the Black Church" that appeared in Charles R. Foster, Ethel R. Johnson, and Grant S. Shockley, *Christian Education Journey of Black Americans: Past, Present, Future* (Nashville: Discipleship Resources, 1985), pages 14-17. In this essay Shockley once again traced the history of black Christian education in American U.S. churches, concluding this time, however, with a clear call to the role of black church education grounded in the wisdom of Black Theology as it was informed by liberation theology and liberative pedagogies.

Black Theology and Christian Education

Black theology confronts Christian education, especially in the black church, with the challenge to engage itself effectively in the liberation of oppressed black people. This challenge has historic significance. It marks the first time in the history of church life in America that a radical minority has aggressively challenged the theological assumptions of the Christian faith on the basis of its own ethic of inclusiveness. Also, it is the first time that a color-minority has articulated such a protest in the form of an alternative system and church style.

In this section of the paper, primary attention will be given to some of the implications of black theologies for Christian education. Christian educators who are black must raise at least two questions in attempting to develop an educational design to complement the current movement of black theology: (1) Why have Christian education in the black church at all? and (2) What are its guidelines?

The rationale for a church education program developed from a black theological perspective is fourfold. First, it is congenial with and "suggests a felt need to reconstruct a world view as it concerns an entire people."[1] That worldview illuminates a new future that black people can have. It is a future in which black people believe and know that they can be free if they want that freedom enough to suffer, sacrifice, and perhaps even die for it. It is the recognition by black people that "we are somebodies."

Second, the agenda of the black community in America is being reshaped to define what that "somebodiness" means—individually, socially, culturally, economically, politically, and theologically. Essentially it calls for the humanization of the dehumanized, the liberation of the oppressed, and the empowerment of the powerless. These are not the kinds of visions that the average white curriculum can handle with much ease. We can no longer "fit into" that curriculum. We must have a curriculum of our own that reflects the uniqueness of becoming Christians in the midst of the black experience in this nation.

Third, the black church has affirmed this agenda in its historic "Black Power Statement": "We commit ourselves as churchmen to make more meaningful in the life of our institutions our conviction that Jesus Christ reigns in the 'here' and 'now' as well as in the future he brings in upon us."[2]

Fourth, the black agenda must begin with black people, and black people must initiate the black agenda. Liberation is not something that can be done *for* a people. In solidarity with others in similar situations—women, Asians, Hispanics, Native Americans—the "consciousness" of black people must be raised, our identity self-affirmed, and our liberation claimed. Implicit in any educational effort is the objective of change. Christian education, therefore, fulfills a highly normative function when it seeks to manipulate the teaching-learning process to the end that justice and a new humanity may emerge.

80

Guidelines for developing the implications of black theology for Christian education in black churches grow out of and center upon the experience, relationships, and situations that black people use in their day-to-day struggle for survival in a basically white-oriented society. In light of this discussion the following guidelines may give direction to a Christian education shaped by the black experience. They must include:

1. A theoretical and operational educational model that is conceptualized as an "empowering process for a powerless" minority. This model turns upside down most education models, which seek to introduce the powerless into the ways of the powerful.

2. A cognitive model of learning that maximizes the biblical, historical, and theological sources and images of the Christian faith as authentically "for others" and pro-black, without being anti-white.

3. A model of learning that is "holistic"; that is, it emphasizes the organic or "whole" nature of existence rather than the compartmentalization of life. It thus ensures and guarantees a wide frame of reference for the inclusion of differences and uniqueness. In other words, pluralism lies at the heart of this alternative approach to Christian education.

4. A model of leadership through which parents, teachers, pastors, and other church leaders can see and be influenced by what Carl Rogers called the development of "fully functioning persons capable of impacting society." In other words, black churchmen and women have to find a "comfortable group" that functions something like the former black Central Jurisdiction of the Methodist Church in raising up leaders for the whole church. Until that time comes when leaders are chosen without any attention to color, there will need to be an opportunity for color-advantaged persons to assume leadership roles of significance.

In summary, let it be said that the objective in curriculum and in teaching the Christian faith in relation to the black experience can best be achieved if viewed from a contextual perspective. That is, we must facilitate the learning of black persons in such ways that they become aware of God as "the God of the oppressed," and of God's self-disclosure in the redemptive and empowering love of Jesus Christ, the liberator; that they may come to know who they are, and what their human situation means, and how they can and may best respond in love and faith through their black Christian experience, personally and socially.

Assumptions

This excerpt was originally published as part of a larger essay entitled "From Emancipation to Transformation to Consummation: A Black Perspective," in Marlene Mayr, ed., *Does the Church Really Want Religious Education?* **(Birmingham: Religious Education Press, 1988), pages 242-46. In this segment of that essay Shockley identifies assumptions he considered to be essential for what he had begun to call an "intentional-engagement" model of Christian religious education grounded in the black church religious experience.**

New Black Church Challenge to Religious Education

The challenge of the black church to religious education is a result of two specific developments in the late 1960s: the eruption of the black revolution and the emergence of the "new" black church. The black revolution was a bold confrontation of the white power structure with black demands for full equality in education, housing, voting, and representational rights. Simultaneously, a cadre of traditional black church leaders, under pressure but also responding to the same cries of the oppressed in the black community, introduced a radically new concept of black church. This new concept brought with it a new understanding of black conditions and black anger in the ghettoes, perceived situations of oppression as clearly related to the mission of the church, and recognized anew the accountability of black churches to black communities. As a result of this, white Protestants and black church traditionalists began to understand issues differently. White Protestants now realized that granting equality to blacks without empowerment was futile. Black church traditionalists came to understand that joining with the black masses in public demonstrations could not be equated with working with them in the "trenches" of the struggle for liberation.

The ambivalence in the old-line black church, and the paralyzing hesitation of "fair-weather" liberals in the white Protestant community, precipitated the issue of the now memorable "Black Power Statement" by progressive black church leaders in July, 1966.[3] This statement which signaled the formal alliance of the black church and the black power movement, declared that conscience and power cannot be separated in the quest for equality. It also made clear to the traditional black church that its energies, resources, and educational efforts in the future must be used more generously and more effectively in the struggle for equality, justice, and peace both in the black community and in the nation.

It was at this point that the new black church was born and the traditional (or "Negro") church died. C. Eric Lincoln summarizes the matter: "The 'Negro Church' that Frazier wrote about no longer exists. It died an agonized death in the harsh turmoil which tried the faith so rigorously, in the decade of the 'Savage Sixties,' for there it had to confront under the most trying circumstances the possibility that 'Negro' and 'Christian' were irreconcilable categories."[4]

New Black Church Ministry

Prior to a discussion of a broad religious education strategy and an overall design to implement the revolutionary goals of the new black church it will be necessary to understand further some of the basic issues and inadequacies of the social theology, direction, strategy, and educational methodology of the traditional black church.

Despite its peaks of high achievement, impressive growth, massive physical façade, and individual giants in leadership throughout its history, the black church prior to the 1960s had not been conspicuous as an institution in the civil rights struggle. The black church often followed rather than led black protest activity and placed institutional growth-aims above missional objectives. It tended to respond more readily to the needs of the affluent than to the cries of the black oppressed in the ghetto. This caused disaffection for the masses and alienation by them. Often communication became *incommunication* making solidarity difficult to accomplish.

Thanks to the National Committee of Black Churchmen's "manifesto" this unfortunate situation changed dramatically. The manifesto affirmed the mission of the new black church. It stated that the gospel is relevant to any situation the black church might face or to which it is expected to respond. In speaking of the shape of the new black church, Gayraud Wilmore did not hesitate to say that secular theology redefines the relationship of the church and the community in such a way that the black church is not only a religious fellowship but also a community organization for liberation.[5]

The resurgence of "a theology of the secular" and its application to the black condition was a prelude to the emergence of a "black theology" first articulated by James H. Cone in his book *Black Theology and Black Power.* This pivotal publication, the first of its kind in American theological thought, clearly established the identity of the black theology movement and shaped the theology in the new black church. Its critical contributions were several: (1) It stimulated reflection on a lost chapter in black religious history; (2) it helped to strengthen a weakened black self-identity and esteem; (3) it called attention to the need for accountability between the black church and the black community; and (4) it greatly influenced black church music and public worship modes toward indigeneity, more congregational participation, spontaneity, responsiveness, and emotional expression.

New Black Church Educational Design

The overall challenge of the new black church to religious education is to assist it in reconstructing its total church-community ministry and relationship to reflect the reuniting of the spiritual-evangelical and the social-liberational intent of the gospel and the historic black church. Several assumptions undergirding this macro-task need to be cited prior to proposing a model and detailing its steps in implementation.

Assumption I: Education for change: The new black church challenges religious education to teach its members to live and minister in and through a church that must be open to changing demands, sensitive to emerging issues, and resilient to shock and reversals. It must also be proactive in relation to change, shaping it for responsible engagement with an open future.

Assumption II: Prophetic education: The new black church challenges religious education to be prophetic, to be continually aware of the black church's responsibility to resist being coopted and exploited as the conservator of the status quo. The black church is always obligated to challenge current values and the "conventional wisdom" and, in the spirit of Jürgen Moltmann, to confront the present as one who shall bring to pass what God has promised in the future.

Assumption III: Education for liberation: Following the thought of Paulo Freire, neutrality in education is a fiction. All education is for either domination or liberation, it cannot be for both. The challenge of the new black church at this point is unmistakably clear. Spirituality, personal salvation or "churchianity" notwithstanding, a major responsibility of the black church has been, is, and will continue to be the humanization of the dehumanized and the liberation of the oppressed.

Assumption IV: Education for mission: Bishop C. D. Coleman stated the "mission assumption" that the new black church should be mission-oriented rather than institution-oriented forthrightly. In a pivotal statement dating from the late 1960s, he admonishes the black church to "cease being preoccupied with its institutional status and image and seize the opportunity to formulate an agenda which will bring the black community to its divine destiny of redeeming and remaking a spiritually denuded society."[6]

Assumption V: Black church genius: Religious education has a key to meet the challenge of the new black church's request to assist it in redefining its mission and ministry. That key, the genius of the black church, historically and always, is relevance. Whatever the real need of the black community has been—survival, protest, consciousness-raising, reform, or revolution—the black church has been there to help.

Intentional Engagement Model

The proposed model to implement the vision of religious education for a liberated and liberating black church is conceptually grounded in: (1) James Cone's *Black Theology of Liberation*; (2) Paulo Freire's liberation praxis theory; and (3) Gayraud S. Wilmore's missional new black church style. The resulting amalgam could be referred to as a black church systemic intentional-engagement model. It comprises several steps which closely parallel Freire's educational philosophy:[7]

Self-Awareness: A primary objective of religious education in black churches should be the development in black persons of an authentic awareness of self-identity, self-determination, and self-direction. The oppressed in general, and blacks in particular, should be taught to regard themselves as objects rather than subjects. While blacks know that authentic existence requires freedom they often fear that freedom as well.

Social Awareness: An equally important religious education objective with blacks is assisting them in developing a growing capacity to perceive the social, political, economic, and political conditions that oppress them daily. Lawrence Jones believes that the black church should and can do something about this through focused preaching, social liturgies, discussion, and experientially guided projects that are relevant and responsive to the real needs of blacks in church and community.

Social Analysis: A third obligation of religious education in black churches is to develop in persons a critical sense. This does not only require a sense of personal and social awareness but also the developed capacity to objectify or transcend specific situations. Only from such a position can the world be viewed with a really critical eye. It is feared that few religious education programs can claim to do this.

Transformation: Blacks must assiduously cultivate capacities for self-awareness, social consciousness, and critical judgment through crucial religious educational experiences in "doing" transformative things in their own lives. The task of religious education in this instance is to provide black role models from churches and communities and elsewhere who exemplify those who are liberated and are practicing it with responsibility.

Praxis: Freire strongly believes that liberation develops from praxis, an action/reflection/action learning procedure which unites learning and action. The curriculum of the black church following this interpretation (not really new in religious education) would be an instantaneous, simultaneous, contemporaneous development of meaningful acts in their struggle against oppression presented for reflection while simultaneously transforming their lives.

Role of the Community: The community plays a significant role in the religious education offered by the black church. It could be, as John Dewey and others have said, the school itself. The community which surrounds the black church could well become the curriculum-planning guide for the church in all of its aspects: preaching, worship, fellowship, teaching, outreach, and social action. Ministries could take their cues from the "generic themes" which they naturally provide.

Challenge from Multiculturalism

Shockley presented this essay, from which the following excerpt was taken, to a consultation on ethnicity in Christian education held on the Scarritt Graduate School campus in Nashville, Tennessee, in the spring of 1985. In this essay Shockley tackles the larger issue of how

to talk about a view of religious education from the black religious experience in the midst of the political dynamics shaping the conversation on multicultural education. In this effort he pushed his earlier discussion of assumptions for a black religious education to an exploration of the foundations for a black religious education. It was published in Charles R. Foster, ed. *Ethnicity in the Education of the Church* (Nashville: Scarritt Press, 1987): 29-39.

Christian Education and the Black Religious Experience

This paper had its origin in the writer's need for a teaching model in a theological seminary that would relate Christian education and the Black religious experience for Black and white ministers who are or will be serving predominately Black congregations and for Black and white ministers who are or will be serving predominately white congregations. I had trouble, however, with the general topic, setting the framework for this consultation and this paper. This difficulty was with the use of the word "ethnicity." Its roots take us back to the Greek word *ethnos*: a people or a population. In its original sense consequently, a reference to an "ethnic" did not involve distinctions based on color. Instead it referred to nations of people dispersed and distributed across the face of the earth. Commonality was based on relationships of kin or tribe, culture, and tradition. If we are not careful in our own social context, we will tend to equate the term *ethnicity* to that wave of immigrants who came to these shores from the northern quadrant of Europe including England. They became the dominant "ethnos" or ethnic group in this new land. With two successive large migrations from northeastern and southeastern Europe, the potential for defining ethnicity in terms of the dominant, and, in this case, white majority population was increased. For all too many this view of a white "ethnos" became identified with a "master" race. Conversations today on ethnicity are influenced by this white majority perspective. The use of the phrase "ethnic minority" as a designation of color underscores the use of ethnicity in this fashion. The issue of an "ethnos" with color distinctions is one with which we must struggle in the pages that follow.

The scarcity of literature and the difficulty one has in locating that which has been written on the Christian education of Black Americans poses a second problem. The literature consists primarily of periodic materials and some research data.[8] The result is that much more research work needs to be done to provide an adequate picture of the richness of the educational dimensions of the Black religious education experience.

The General Situation

White Christians in the United States, after having evangelized and converted Blacks to a "catholic" and "inclusive" Church in the eighteenth and nineteenth centuries, immediately and almost universally denied them full access and/or equality of fellowship in local communities of faith. The result of this anomalous situation in the twentieth century (indeed in 1986!) is the presumptuous and infamous presence of color segregated Christian congregations, Sunday schools, and educational programs on a nationwide basis. The Black Christian response to this dilemma in Christian racial relations ethics has basically been of two kinds. Vast numbers of Black Christians withdrew in protest from white churches and formed Black churches and/or independent denominations together with indigenous programs of Christian education. Blacks who remained in white churches and/or white denominations generally accepted the assimilationist perspective of the white majority churches in matters of faith, worship, church order, and Christian education.

For this latter group the Civil Rights movement of the late 1950s, the "Freedom Now" movement of the early 1960s, the Black Power movement of the closing years of that decade, the Black Liberation movement of the early 1970s, and the current tendency of the churches not to venture beyond the prudent and protected confines of local, state, and/or national legal decisions or community consensus, have raised new insistent and unprecedented questions. The dilemma for these church members may be traced to the fact that they have followed a secular rather than a radical Christian theological position. Their churches joined the civil rights bandwagon culminating in the "resolution" of the legal problems of segregation. These churches thereby concluded that their problems had been solved. But when their members begin to discuss anything having to do with the relationship of the races beyond the structures of institutions or legal integration, people hardly know what they are talking about. The discussion of inclusiveness from a theological and ethical perspective has not yet been seriously engaged. We consequently are faced with two important questions. The first is theological: Is there not a rationale for inclusiveness beyond civil or ecclesiastical litigation? The second is practical. Is there not a process by which an inclusive Christian education can be accomplished, given the commitment and intentionality of many churches and their leaders?

A Definition of the Problem

The problem that this situation presents and the problem this paper will attempt to resolve is twofold: how to rationalize, conceptualize, strategize, and implement a Christian education program that has integrity and viability in relationship to both the Christian faith and the Black experience; and how to work at this problem among predominantly Black churches in predominantly white denominations.

This twofold problem reduces itself further to several questions: (1) What is the nature and purpose of the church and what does it have to do with the issue of race? This question has rarely been addressed comprehensively throughout the history of the church. (2) What is the Christian position regarding racial and/or ethnic inclusiveness? And must the definitions arising from that position be confused by the church's experience in the United States in which assimilation has dominated the majority group's attitudes toward minorities and reinforced the supremacy of white ethnicity? (3) And what should be the role of the church toward persons who are discriminated against, oppressed, and/or disadvantaged?

Foundations for Christian Education in Relation to the Black Experience

Five foundations undergird the reconstruction of Christian education in mainline Protestant denominations in the United States when the Black religious experience is taken seriously: (1) the history of the Sunday school movement, especially between 1875 and 1935; (2) the socio-cultural milieu of racism, which informs and deforms Black personality; (3) the biblical-theological roots of Black liberation theology and Christian racial inclusiveness; (4) an educational philosophy compatible with liberation theology; and (5) the psychological issues in Black personality development.

THE HISTORICAL FOUNDATION

The Sunday school movement in the United States never effectively related itself to the Black experience. Nor did it ever show more than a token interest in an inclusive approach to Blacks. The vast majority of English and other missionaries serving in the American English colonies withdrew at the close of the Revolutionary War. This left the missionizing and evangelizing of Blacks (and Indians) to the emerging denominations in the new nation. While there was no lack of enthusiasm to continue the work of organizations such as the Society for the Propagation of the Gospel, the direction of this development in Christian education in relation to Blacks perpetuated the movement toward segregated Sunday schools.

There were other distressing developments in the Sunday school movement in relation to Blacks. Some white patrons of Sunday schools were concerned that slaves might learn more than the restricted and innocuous biblical material requisitioned for them by slaveholders. Consequently the Bible was literally taken apart and put back together again to phase out or re-phrase any passage with "freedom" implications. The objective of the American Sunday School Union's "Mississippi Valley Enterprise," however, never reached the Blacks of the region. As a matter of fact between 1830 and 1890 little or nothing was done for the religious education of Blacks in the Mississippi Valley, despite the fact that this section comprised one of the most densely populated Black areas in the country. This "by-pass" was characteristic of the operational style of the American Sunday School Union, particularly during the slavery era. Lawrence N. Jones, Dean of Howard University School of Religion, has suggested that the American Sunday School Union as well as the American Tract Society and the America Bible Society ignored "the whole issue of slavery in order not to alienate those slave holders who offered financial support."[9]

Consequently the main thrust and motif in the Christian education offered to Blacks during slavery and especially from 1800 onward was not "religious" or "Christian" really but rather sub-Christian and diversionary. Prohibited by the "black codes" from gathering or being gathered together as a group to learn to read or write, much Christian education from about 1834 was relegated to what historian Carter G. Woodson calls "religion without letters" or oral (catechetical) instruction.

In summary, it may be said that early efforts toward the Christian education of Blacks grew out of the mission impulse. This motive was subverted however, by the equivocation of the churches on the issue of human and political rights of chattel slaves. Although Christian education among Blacks antedates any other organized effort to improve the slave's condition of illiteracy, much of this education involved a truncated version of the biblical message accommodated to the requirement of slaveholders. It also assumed Black intellectual inferiority. The (white) Sunday school movement moreover, did not relate itself to Blacks in helpful or effective ways. It showed only token interest in inclusive schools and failed consistently to come to terms with its racist policies and practices. Much of the formal religious education Blacks received through white church sponsorship has perpetuated, in other words, distortions of classical theological understandings of the relationship of baptism and the unity of the Church as the Body of Christ. Black church education has consequently been shaped significantly by patterns of white racism and white ethnic dominance.

THE SOCIO-CULTURAL FOUNDATION

Perhaps the best way to understand the racist socio-cultural milieu in which Black personality developed and which instructs any educational program that would "uplift" them is to identify and list several contemporary influences adversely affecting Black people:

1. The rise in Black unemployment and the distressing level of Black *under*employment.
2. Cutbacks in government-supported human development and welfare programs.
3. The growing disparity between Black and white income.
4. The prospect that Blacks are three times as likely to be poor as whites.
5. The negative effect of inflation on Black people more so than on white people.
6. The development of anti-affirmative-action attitudes among whites of all classes.
7. The general public decline of interest in Black concerns.
8. The new "preferred" concern for other ethnic needs and women's needs when they are used as a diversionary tactic to avoid addressing Black needs.
9. The none too subtle resegregation of the public schools.

10. The comparatively lower quality of education available in the public schools which most Black children and youth attend.
11. The increase in alcohol and drug abuse in the Black community.
12. The rising cost and inaccessibility of quality medical services to poor Blacks.
13. The nefarious practice of "redlining" by the housing and real estate industries.
14. Cuts in federal aid to Black college students.
15. The scarcity of adequate housing for many non-affluent Black people.
16. The increased poor communication between Blacks and whites at all levels.

Added to these concerns are the following indicators of the lack of real inclusiveness of Blacks in national life:

1. The increased Black presence in the cities has not been accompanied by a comparable increase in political and economic influence and/or power.
2. The increased isolation of Black and white into city and suburb.
3. The under-representation by Blacks in most significant levels of decision making in civic and white church power centers.

THE BIBLICAL-THEOLOGICAL FOUNDATION

In relating Christian education to the Black religious experience, care must be taken to preserve the integrity of both the Christian faith and the Black experience. The language and conceptualizations found in Black theology have begun this process. A Christian education informed by Black theology can thereby become the means whereby liberation and humanization themes are heard and practiced in the Black community by the congregation with the care, guidance, and support of pastors. Black theology confronts Christian education, especially in the Black church, with the challenge to engage itself effectively in the liberation of oppressed people. This challenge has historic significance. It marks the first time in the history of church life in the United States that a racial minority has aggressively challenged the theological assumptions of the Christian faith on the basis of its own ethic. Also, it is the first time that a color-minority has articulated such a protest in the form of an alternative system and church style. With this in mind Christian educators who are Black, or who are interested in considering the Black religious experience as they "do" Christian education, must raise a basic question in attempting to develop an educational design that faithfully reflects and complements Black theology. That basic question has to do with the relation of the church to the world, that is, to all of God's people in the world!

The rationale then for a church education program developed from a Black theological perspective is threefold. First, it is congenial with and "suggests a felt need to reconstruct a world view as it concerns an entire people."[10] It begins with the assumption that we are all a part of God's kingdom. That worldview illuminates a new future that Black people can claim. It is a future in which Black people can believe. They know they can be free if they want that freedom badly enough to suffer and sacrifice for it.

Second, the agenda of the Black community in the United States is redefining what "somebodiness" means—individually, socially, culturally, economically, politically, and theologically. Essentially it calls for the humanization of the dehumanized, the liberation of the oppressed and the empowerment of the powerless. These are not the kind of terms that the average "white" curriculum can handle with much ease. We can no longer "fit into" such curriculum. We must have a curriculum that reflects the uniqueness of becoming Christians in the midst of the Black experience in this nation until that experience is transformed!

Third, the Black church has affirmed this agenda in its historic (1966) "Black Power Statement": "We commit ourselves as churchmen to make meaningful in the life of our institutions our conviction that Jesus Christ reigns in the 'here' and 'now' as well as in the future he brings in upon us."[11]

. Hence, the Black church has a unique mission. That mission is to assist Black and all other people in the struggle for liberation from dehumanization, depersonalization, desocialization, and disempowerment. That mission is to help Black and all people to "overcome" instead of "giving up." Jesus put it well in the Gospel of Luke (4:18-19 KJV): "The Spirit of the Lord is upon me, because he hath anointed me to preach the gospel to the poor; he hath sent me to heal the brokenhearted, to preach deliverance to the captives, and recovering of sight to the blind, to set at liberty them that are bruised, To preach the acceptable year of the Lord."

THE PHILOSOPHICAL FOUNDATION

Any philosophical foundation for an approach to Christian education in relation to the Black experience must necessarily be compatible with the insights of Black theology. The educational philosophy of Paulo Freire in his landmark book, *The Pedagogy of the Oppressed*, most nearly does this. And yet, for a philosophy of Christian education that is relevant for the Black religious experience, it is necessary to move beyond Freire to identify several assumptions and stages of implementation integral to the model we are developing.

Five assumptions inform this model. First, the involvement of the church in education affirms its intent to enable persons to engage the ethic of the church with the realities of their situations in life. The educational process is thereby highly interactive, engaging learners with both life situations and churchly traditions and teachings. Second, this involvement further indicates the acceptance of the continuing challenge to the church community to the oppressed and to work with them in solidarity for liberation. This is the liberating perspective described by Freire. It involves the translation of theory into practice. Third, church education has an incarnational mission in the world. That mission is "a transforming process here and now." Such a process may have to reach beyond "reformation" to "revolution" for accomplishment. Fourth, education for Christian living is a humanizing process, enabling constructive growth and removing obstructive factors as it seeks to discover with persons ways to maximize their "humanness." Fifth, church education is always affirmative. It is never neutral. It is education for the oppressed against the oppressor—who is also oppressed—that both may be sensitized to aid in restructuring church, school, and society. This educational model is therefore for all Christians who intentionally engage in a community of all ethnics to become the new church that moves into the future.

There are several stages or levels involved in the "Freire method" of liberation learning. First, a new consciousness which allows the oppressed to identify the kind of "prescribed" reality that is being perceived. Critical awareness of their dehumanization by oppressors must be seen for what it really is. The "ontological vocation" of personhood, to become human, a "subject" rather than a mere "object," active in determining one's destiny rather than passive, must be every person's agenda-priority. Freire says, this is not "given" to persons by their oppressors but it must be "taken." Second, the creation of this consciousness needs the support of community and dialogue. A setting in which persons, as co-equals, can teach and learn from each other in dialogical conversation is basic to combating the "culture of silence" which has conditioned the oppressed not to speak of or actively attempt to become liberated from their oppression. This escalation of perspective from "object" to "subject" is a prelude to "conscientization" or the developing capacity of persons to perceive an entire syndrome of contradictions that comprise their oppression and dehumanized state. At this point they begin to see some of the larger issues of economic, political, social, and cultural realities that are oppressive.

The center of education for liberation occurs when persons are able to utilize their capacities of self-transcendence to evaluate reality, and as subjects, of naming the world instead of being named by it. Here the action of posing problems through dialogical learning-teaching leads people into the ability to change rather than merely to cope with situations; to attack a problem to the end that its solution might enhance personal identity and social destiny, rather than to be a part of the problem.

THE PSYCHOLOGICAL FOUNDATION

The psychological foundations for Christian education that are related to the Black religious experience grow out of the central problem of being Black in a white-dominated society. Being Black in the United States perennially presents the problem of being different. This experience is problematic not because of the high visibility of color, but because of what color implies. Being Black in a white-oriented and white-dominated society means being thought of as "inferior." It culminates in victimization via prejudice, segregation, and discrimination. When these patterns are experienced in, through, and by the church and its institutions and agencies such as the Sunday school and youth groups, questions of self-esteem, acceptance, the credibility of the gospel, and a host of other questions arise.

This anomalous situation, faced to a greater or lesser degree in the United States by all persons of any visible African ancestry, has engendered in the psyche of Black people a highly articulated self-consciousness, often a hypersensitivity, but invariably a sense of a dual existence. W. E. B. DuBois, in *The Souls of Black Folk* calls it "twoness": "One ever feels his twoness,—an American, A Negro; two souls, two thoughts, two unreconciled strivings; two warring ideals in one dark body, whose dogged strength alone keeps it from being torn asunder."[12]

Summarily, this is the Black experience. It is the life and world of any and all people of color who must or will identify themselves as being of

African descent. It is the ever present reality of knowing and feeling and living as a nonwhite in a white-oriented and white-controlled society. It is the Black group experience, historic and present, of being oppressed, disdained, deprived, excluded, alienated, neglected, and rejected.

The implication of the Black experience for Christian education derives not only from the fact that the earliest attitudes held toward Blacks were, almost without exception, at best paternalistic, and at worst, racist, but also from the fact that through it all Black people demonstrated the capacity to hold these two estimations in tension, selecting what was necessary to survive as persons from the white Christian model that was presented to them in a perverted fashion and rejecting the concepts of white Christians which sought to destroy their every vestige of self-worth and respect.

This plight of the Black American, who J. Saunders Reddings says "[lives] constantly on two planes of awareness," was not only one of personal rejection but one of social and religious segregation as well. As Winthrop D. Jordan observes in *White Over Black*: "The Negro's color sets him radically apart from Englishmen. It also served as a highly visible label identifying the natives of a distant continent which for ages Christians had known as a land of men radically defective in religion."[13]

There are several significant implications for a Christian education among Black people that derive from this "splitness" or double-visioned perspective. This dual identity-existence of Black people influenced their religious development historically and presently. It was the existential situation in which Black theological belief systems developed. In Black sermons, spirituals, prayers, and teachings in Sunday schools, Black people came to terms with their blackness, their expressional gifts, and their social situation of slavery and other forms of brutalizing oppression in a white racist church and society. Here is where they worked out their salvation in relation to the questions of their bondage, their separation from family members, their chattel status, their ideas of good, evil, God, and Satan.

The church came to have a particular significance for Black people in slavery times (and ever since) as it provided them with a gathered community of relative freedom, expressional outlet, community information, group solidarity, personal affirmation, mutual aid, and leadership development. The Black community then, grew up around and was influenced more by the Black church than any other single institution. As a central meeting place, a platform for the promulgation of ideas, a likely place to hear of a job, a basic meeting place for youth, and an educational institution, it was unrivaled as a center of power and community. Further, if it is remembered that little if any direction was given to the moral and ethical development of Black people by any other institution prior to Emancipation, the large influence of the church in the Black experience must be regarded as singular.

In short, the Black church became the first institution in the Black community that dealt seriously with the split identity crisis of the comprehensive black-white dichotomy in North America. The significance of this fact cannot be underestimated for Christian education. The Black preacher and the Black church were of inestimable aid to Black people in their negotiating the identity crisis of their "twoness" by providing the churches the kind of preaching, worship, activities, and programs which supported their groping efforts to affirm their identities, worth, and aspirations as human beings and as children of God. The church has been the primary educator in the Black community in that situation. It is this role of the church that must currently be addressed as we consider the Christian education of Black children, youth, and adults today.

The Challenge of Religious Pluralism

This excerpt from "Religious Pluralism and Religious Education: A Black Protestant Perspective," edited by Norma H. Thompson, in *Religious Pluralism and Religious Education* (Birmingham: Religious Education Press, 1988), pages 152-61, extends insights Shockley began to explore during and immediately after his international travels with the Board of Missions of The United Methodist Church introduced him to the inter-religious struggles and encounters in many nations of the developing world. Since our attention is directed to his quest for a model of religious education we have not included the introductory sections of this essay in this volume. They lay out his understanding of religious pluralism in general. Instead we pick up on his discussion where he begins to identify and draw implications from that general introduction for the religious education of African Americans. In this effort he identifies in the pluralism of the black religious experience insights relevant to the development of a model for Christian religious education responsive to the national and global context of all American Christians.

Achieving Common Human Goals

No single word better characterizes the nature of the international situation or forecasts the shape of international relations than the term
interdependence. Mutual dependence, however, does not ensure mutual
trust, the necessary basis of effective interdependent relations. Only deep
understanding, respect, equality of status, and personal security can do
that. Arnold Toynbee correctly observed: "Human beings have had six
thousand years to become strangers to one another, and now we have
hardly any time at all for learning the most difficult art of dwelling
together in unity." Pursuant to this, the role of religious education in relation to the insistent reality of interdependence and the yet distant real
pluralism of faiths, internationally, is critical. Its task is to equip persons—cognitively, affectively, and behaviorally—to discover, analyze,
reflect upon, decide, act out, and celebrate, individually as Christians and
corporately as the church, some of the universal themes, first principles,
and prime values of the Christian faith. A second objective is to clarify,
instruct, reconcile, and attempt to resolve specific common human issues
that are facing our "global village." Hopefully, this will also witness to
unities and harmonies that were never thought to exist through diversi-
ties and discontinuities that have existed and will exist.

Dialogue is best suited to begin to achieve the objectives that have
been outlined. As defined by Paul Knitter and as it will be used in this
chapter it is "the exchange of experience and understanding between two
or more partners with the intention that all partners grow in experience
and understanding."[14] Dialogue at this dimension is more than protracted
discussion, a mere exchange of opinion. It is a philosophy of education, a
way of knowing and doing (praxis), and a theological dialectic, simultaneously. Preeminently, however, it is transformational! Knitter details
three presuppositions to dialogue that are germane for its educational use.
It must be based on "personal religious experience and firm truth-claims."
It must also be based on "the recognition of the possible truth in all religions . . . grounded in the hypothesis of a common ground and a goal for
all religions." It must be based on "openness to the possibility of
change/conversion."[15] The basic educational design that is being proposed here is an extrapolation of the particularistic language, that is, religion, in the model and the redeployment of the paradigm in relation to
other common human issues "in the concern of all religions to promote
the unity of humanity and to offset the danger of world destruction."[16]

The other issues recommended for dialogue are: humanization and human rights; environment; peace and justice; population/hunger/poverty; and racial justice. Such a program is based on the growing awareness of an increasing number of religionists and theologians that theology as we know and do it today must now be written from within a world religious perspective.

Pluralism and the Black Experience: Excursions in Exclusion

Color prejudice, historically and presently, has excluded black Americans from the ethnic-diversity and ethnic pluralist dialogue and rendered them the most unassimilable racial group in the nation. Black people have been aware of this from time immemorial. And no one has expressed it better than the venerated black bard and scholar, W. E. B. DuBois who in speaking of the isolation of black people from the general society said: "One ever feels his two-ness—an American, a Negro; two souls, two thoughts, two unreconciled strivings; two warring ideals in one dark body, whose dogged strength alone keeps it from being torn asunder."[17] This has been the case as far back as one chooses to go in American history. The Declaration of Independence (1776) in its famed statement about the equality of all men ignored the existence of hundreds of thousands of black human beings who were then slaves. Sanction for the continuance of slavery was written into the heart of the Constitution of the nation (1787). In one sentence, not superseded until the ratification of the Fourteenth Amendment (1868), black people were accounted only as "three-fifths of all other persons." Fugitive slave laws had federal approbation until slavery was abolished in 1865. The United States Supreme Court by its Dred Scott decision said in effect that black people had no rights that white people had to respect. Following the Civil War it was necessary to free blacks from bondage, declare them citizens, and grant them the right to vote. Despite these legal protections in 1896 the Supreme Court decided in the Plessy-Ferguson case that separate treatment for blacks is equal. It would be 1954 before another Supreme Court would say that separate is inherently unequal. There is a fundamental lesson for all in this overview of the treatment of black people, one of the nation's several color-minorities. While blacks have been one of the ethnically diverse groups in what became a "plural" society, they have never been (and are not now) really considered to be equal to other diverse ethnic groups. Their relation to American "pluralism" has always carried a negative valence in combination with nonblack or noncolored ethnic group elements.

Black Americans have not only been denied equality as persons; they have also been denied acceptance as individuals and as an entire racial group. Larger than any other ethnic grouping in the nation, their status is basically governed by their racial identification. The rationale for this is the tacit practice of a policy of assimilation in reference to racial minorities in this country. The Anglo-Conformity sub-thesis of this theory, originally applicable to immigrants and rife with overtones of non-white inferiority, blatantly asserts the superiority of Anglo-Saxon culture and lifestyles and presents this as the nonnegotiable basis for becoming an American. The melting-pot sub-thesis, also originally intended to apply to nonblack immigrants, espoused a "blending of cultures" approach to assimilation with an intermarriage component. Cultural pluralism, the third model, was a "functional integration of people into the economic and political order of the dominant society while they retain a distinctive cultural and institutional life."[18] In reference to black people all three of these theories, and the concept of assimilation itself, were and are patently dysfunctional. They were designed to accommodate immigrants (and others) to a system with exploitive objectives and aggressively dominant motivations. The very simple reason why they are generally dysfunctional for black people and other color-minorities is the fact that blacks are at best only marginally related to the system!

Black objections to the various patterns of acculturation just discussed come under three general headings: goals, objectives, and strategy. Increasingly black people were asking about receding goals despite more than four decades of focused struggle. Progress had been made in voting rights, housing, education, and public accommodation privileges, but as the goals were approached intransigence, backlash, and a reactionary White House administration caused the goals to recede. The objectives of equality, identity, integrity, self-determination, and empowerment, so right and so clear in the 1960s and 1970s, seemed ambiguous and difficult to achieve in the 1980s. Likewise strategy again became an issue. Must we accommodate to the power system and to the open "tokenism" route or remain in the trenches and fight the good fight of liberation for our brothers and sisters? For better or for worse it seems that the way ahead for blacks in America is the honing of our own skills and the solidification of our own community and the extension of the struggle for liberation all in the context of the "two-ness" of our hyphenated America. In any event, most black people knew that despite any moderate success the assimilation approach may have had in pushing a few blacks ahead, the approach itself was bankrupt and must be replaced by one that is far more just in administering equity, inclusive in outreach, and more pluralist in principle.

Pluralism and Black Churches

Has religious pluralism affected the black church differently than cultural pluralism affected the black community? Does the fact that there is a Black Church of black churches comprising almost twenty million black Christians not attest loudly to the fact that it is a separate diversity not yet pluralized? Black religion and the black church in the United States have historically been assigned an inferior status in relation to white religion and white churches. Winthrop Jordan observes: "The Negro's color set him radically apart from Englishmen. It also served as a highly visible label identifying the motives of a distant continent which for ages Christians had known as a land of men radically defective in religion."[19] Not only have black people been considered spiritually inferior to whites but they were unwanted as fellow church members. The cycle of nonacceptance is well known: (1) white conversion of blacks: (2) white rejection of blacks as fellow church members; (3) the rise of separate black services; (4) the development of separate black churches, in protest and out of a sense of deep frustration; and (5) continued discriminatory treatment of blacks who remained in white churches. What were the radical dynamics operating in this situation? Briefly, most early American black converts (including Native Americans) were in biracial or triracial churches. As these groups developed into settled congregations requiring primary social contacts, peer relations, and equality of treatment, covert racism became overt and segregation patterns became the standard rule and practice. By World War I (1914–18) the nadir in the church segregation of blacks from whites had been reached despite protests from blacks and some whites. Racial segregation, long practiced in the nation, had been sanctioned by the churches. Between World Wars I and II and until the United States Supreme Court *Brown vs. Board of Education* decision outlawing segregation in the public schools (1954), the situation did not really improve. Frank Loescher, in speaking of this period says: "The record of its policies and practices makes it evident that in many respects it (the church) has contributed to the seriousness of the very problem it should be helping to solve."[20]

Not only did the black church have grave reservations about white lack of respect for its religious heritage and equality of personhood, it also had ample reason to question their real interest in engaging the systematic causes of racism during the Civil Rights era. At the peak of the struggle for equal rights in the nation, the churches hardly moved beyond tokenism. In the midst of talks about church unions, mergers, and cooperation, blacks and other minorities were "power pawns" rather than self-determining power agents. An examination of white support during the rights movement revealed deceptive attempts to "contain" the struggle and defuse its power. Loyalty gave way to arid legalism. Opportunities were offered without the advantages needed to exploit them: Symbolic status was given in the place of substantial authority. Summarily, there was little evidence or hope, then or now, that the objectives of religious pluralism, namely, peer relationships, self-determination, and empowerment would or could ever be achieved. In other words, white pluralism would mean more white racial supremacy, more and more subtle oppression, more defunct assimilation, less justice but more jails, greater tolerance but less dialogue.

With this experiential background it is not strange that the black church's first question in relation to religious pluralism is not its philosophy, objective, or design but its integrity and intentionality. It must know that this venture into religious pluralism would not involve it in another assimilation game in which it would be denied equality, authentic participation, and decision-making power and become comic characters in a glorified "integration" charade.

Religious Pluralism and the Black Church: The New Paradigm in Black

Powerful forces, urgent needs, and persistent leadership in both the black community and in the black churches in the late 1960s generated the demand for a new framework in which to do further problem solving in reference to continuing black marginalization, exclusion, and disempowerment. The quest was for a new black paradigm that would articulate concepts, assumptions, methods, and strategies for the social, religious, economic, and political liberation of black people. This desire for a new direction was even more significant because it was based on black community consensus. The black masses were still hopeful for a response to their dire plight. Former assimilationist advocates for whom integration was a great disenchantment and for whom real equality was still a myth were ready to try something new. Black activists were characteristically impatient to move! Prior to exploring the new black church paradigm, however, a closer look at these sets of events, some pluralistically oriented, are necessary. These event-sets relate to the black church, black theology, and the pluralization of black theology.

The Black Church

The black revolution, beginning in the late 1950s inspired the radicalization of the black church. An organizing convocation for this purpose, held in the 1960s, committed the black church to the black liberation movement. In 1966 a group of black church leaders issued the now historic "Black Power Statement,"[21] reaffirming solidarity with the Black Power Movement and reprimanding white churches for suggesting that black people should only seek power in passive ways. Somewhat later another statement was made, "The Urban Mission in a Time of Crisis," making it very clear that the black church would no longer tolerate being "by-passed" by the power deputies of white church structures in their work in black communities. In pluralist style it insisted that a peer relationship must pertain in any negotiations, transaction of ideas or strategies or funding in the black community. Worship and music in the black church was reviewed to ensure and encourage their reflection of the style and quality of the diverse black modes of worship.

The black theology movement, one of the few unique American contributions to the field of theology, though beginning in a rudimentary form in the nineteenth century, formally came into existence in 1967. *The Report of the Theological Committee of the National Committee of Black Churchmen* spoke to the need for the contextualization of black theology since this had not been done and obviously would not be done by the white theological community. At this same meeting whites (and others) were taken to task for denigrating black religion. The first publication of the movement was James H. Cone's *Black Theology and Black Power* (Seabury Press, 1969). A second phase in black theological inquiry began in 1970 with the organization of the Society for the Study of Black

Religion, a forum for theological dialogue and black theological education professional interests.

The pluralization of black theology began almost with the black theology movement itself and continues to the present. Dialogues, conversations, and/or visits have taken place in Africa, Asia, Latin America, and North America. This probably makes black theology one of the most highly pluralized theologies of recent times. The continental profile is interesting:

Africa:

Ivory Coast (1969): Conference and initiation of Pan-African Skills Project to recruit technically skilled Afro-Americans for work and service in Africa sponsored by the All-Africa Conference of Churches;

Tanzania (1897): The first formal dialogue produced Black Faith and Black Solidarity compiled and edited by Priscilla Massie (New York: Friendship Press, 1973);

Ghana (1974): The Society for the Study of Black Religion and the All-Africa Conference of Churches Consultation discussion of John Mbiti's controversial paper, "An African Views American Black Theology" and Bishop Desmond Tutu's rejoinder, "Black Theology/African Theology—Soul Mates or Antagonists";

Ghana (1977): Pan-Africa Conference of Third World Theologians in which James H. Cone responded to John Mbiti's paper and moved the dialogue to a Third World context.

Latin America:

Switzerland (1973): Symposium: Black Theology and Latin American Liberation Theology;

USA (1975): Detroit Conference on Theology in the Americas;

Mexico (1977): Conference: Encounter of Theologians;

Cuba (1979): Consultation: Evangelization and Politics: A Black Perspective.

Asia:

Dialogues have not taken place in Asia on a consultation basis. James Cone has spoken there on several occasions and was well-received. His comment is that the Koreans are quite sensitive to the racial issue in the United States. Japanese Christians were found to be "more concerned with Euro-American theologians of the West than addressing the oppression of Koreans or of the poor generally."[22]

New Black Church Paradigm

The new black church paradigm is an exemplary model of the promise and fulfillment of religious pluralism in two ways, theoretically and practically. Theoretically, based on the pluralist philosophy that truth ultimately has more than one valid construction and human thinking can approach these constructions in different ways, black theology challenges the notion that European-American theologizing is the only valid construction. Conversely, it affirms that theologizing can and must be done by black people from a black perspective. Second, asserting with John B. Cobb that "nothing historical is absolute and any tendency to absolutize any feature of Christianity is idolatry,"[23] black theology challenges a historic theological position that disputes the validity of its claims and affirms that it is and ought to be a theology of the oppressed. Third, granted the pluralist principle that the thought enterprise should seek to incorporate various insights into new, larger, and more functional entities by combining and recombining concepts rather than fabricating reductionist syncretisms, black theology affirms the pluralist principle of free-standing inclusivism rather than elective assimilation.

At the practical level religious pluralism has similar implications. Following the general principle of "plural" validity, black theology rejects the notion that "liberation" is limited to a single context or a simple approach. It affirms the sensibility of exploring any and all potentially relevant means of liberating the oppressed. James Cone, for an example, would probably agree with Walter Watson's statement on this point: "The history of philosophy is now seen less as a museum of curiosities and errors and more as an inventory of archetypal possibilities that supply standards and resources for future inquiries."[24]

With this abbreviated explanation of the theoretical basis of the new black church paradigm, we can now move to a discussion of the principle features of the model (for religious education) it suggests.

Rationale: Black theology and a radicalized black church emerged from the 1970s as critical and timely responses to the black revolution for equality, identity, and self-determination. They also present themselves as viable alternatives to white Christianity and white American theology both of which have historically held black religion to be "defective." Further, black theology and the black church was also a response to either the unwillingness or the inability of white Protestantism to offer more than rhetoric to the challenge of their own theology of inclusiveness. This intransigence mandated the black church to develop a new black church style demonstrating a pluralist as well as a holistic approach to a ministry with the oppressed. This new paradigm presents itself as an autonomous, freestanding system emphasizing:

1. "The renewal and enhancement of the black church in terms of its liturgical life, its theological interpretation (and), its understanding of its mission."
2. "The development of the black church, not only as a religious fellowship, but as a community organization . . . which uses its resources . . . to address the problems of . . . the black community."
3. "The projection of a new quality of church life which would equip and strengthen the church as custodian and interpreter of that cultural heritage which is rooted in the peculiar experience of black people . . . and the faith that has sustained them."
4. "The contribution of the black church, out of its experience of suffering and the yearning for freedom, of that quality of faith, hope, and love which can activate, empower, renew, and unite the whole church of Christ."[25]

Primary Characteristics

The following discussion of the characteristics in an "intentional-engagement model" for Christian education in the black church is from an essay entitled "Black Pastoral Leadership in Religious Education," in Robert L. Browning, ed., *The Pastor as Religious Educator* (Birmingham: Religious Education Press, 1989), pages 201-6. In this essay Shockley elaborates on the themes in "an intentional-engagement model" of religious education introduced earlier and makes even more explicit his reliance on Black Theology as the primary source and inspiration for this thinking.

An Intentional-Engagement Model

This final section of the chapter will suggest a social justice ministry perspective and model that has grown out of the black church. Basically, it is one that "worked" as the black community in concert with the black church cooperated to initiate and support the unprecedented revolution in civil rights for black people during 1955–70. This model has the potential for adaptation by any church if it becomes committed to and intentionally involved in a social justice ministry in solidarity with the oppressed. Essentially, it is a model that relates mission and ministry in "praxis" through the change agency of the church. The characteristic-objectives of this "intentional-engagement model" are six: (1) biblical integrity; (2) radical contextuality; (3) systematic engagement; (4) educational change; (5) programmatic integration; and (6) laity empowerment.[26] Prior to describing this intentional-engagement model, two distinctions should immediately be recognized as significant variables in relation to its evaluation and/or deployment. First, black people needed justice ministries because of their immediate and existential situation(s) of oppression and their deathless determination to correct and transcend it. Whites and white churches while deploring the oppressive situation of millions of black people were not directly the victims of oppression. Their involvement in liberation acts was qualified and different. Second, generally white churches have difficulty relating faith and social action. Their people may participate in "studies," "research," and "mission" projects but seldom in movements for systemic change, that is, for the correction of the root causes of the problems themselves. Actually, very little in their background prepares them to engage the many "principalities and powers" that cause systemic injustice. Third, church members find it difficult to interrelate personal faith and social change. Regarding this dilemma, however, Gustavo Gutierrez maintains that it is not possible for a Christian to say that "he lives on the level of liberation from sin or sonship and brotherhood if he is disinterested in economic, social, and political liberation."

Characteristic 1: Biblical Integrity

The biblical story and witness has perennially been a prime source and central foundation for black Christians in their quest of freedom, dignity, and equality. It has also been a mainstay in black church preaching, worship, music, and teaching, as well as the motivator for evangelism, mission, and service.

The black religious experience is replete with Old and New Testament references and images of God's concern for justice, righteousness, and their freedom from slavery. In the life, teachings, and ministry of Jesus, black churches stress his concern for human need, his solidarity with the poor, his association with the outcast, and his identification with the marginal people of society.

Crucially important in the understanding of the black church in relation to the Bible are its convictions: that God is the Lord of history; that God is concerned about and involved in history; that God is the God of the oppressed whom God came to liberate in Jesus Christ, and now through the black church.

Characteristic II: Radical Contextuality

The black church, historically and currently, has held reflection and action in creative tension. It acts, believing that the activity of God primarily occurs in the midst of the trials and tribulations of the poor, oppressed, prisoners, and outcasts. Theologian James Cone makes this the basic definition of black theology referring to it as "that theology which arises out of the need to articulate the significance of black presence in a hostile white world. It is black people reflecting religiously on the black experience, attempting to redefine the relevance of the Christian gospel for their lives."[27] William Jones makes this same point when he says, "Each black theology presents itself, implicitly or explicitly, as a specific strategy for black liberation. From this perspective it must be regarded as an 'engaged' or committed theology, for it makes a prior commitment to an ultimate goal, i.e., transforming from oppression to authentic humanity."[28]

Characteristic III: Systematic Engagement

Biblical integrity and radical contextualization lead to another characteristic of the intentional-engagement model for social justice ministries—systematic engagement, that is, identifying, analyzing, correcting, or eliminating restraining destructive structures and/or systems that support and sustain oppression, racism, and sexism. Herbert Richardson indicates that this was a major concern for Martin Luther King Jr. throughout the civil rights struggle: "King's perception of the human problem . . . led him to emphasize . . . that his struggle was directed against the forces, or structures of evil itself rather than against the person or group who is doing the evil."[29] The authenticity and effectiveness of the civil rights movement, largely the fruit of King's leadership, was due to this assessment of the fundamental problem and the development of a complementary strategy of nonviolence to resist evil and witness to good.

Characteristic IV: Educational Change

Two basic issues emerge whenever the educational philosophy that is implicit in the civil rights movement or Martin Luther King's leadership is discussed. Those issues are purpose and method. Can a religious education that resists social change, as frequently charged,[30] be useful in initiating, advocating, and inculcating social justice teachings and action? If this issue can be resolved, what methodology best serves this purpose?[31]

Religious education can become an ally of social justice ministries rather than serving merely as "social cement" or "legitimization" for the maintenance of a traditionalist religious establishment. According to Peter Berger what is needed to reverse this anomalous situation is a religious education that challenges—through praxis—and remains "dysfunctional" rather than "functional" for those who would domesticate its radically prophetic message. Berger makes this point quite clear in the following statement: "The family-centered and child-centered religiosity of many of our suburban middle-class churches contributes greatly to this problem. The ideology of religious education . . . gives intellectual rationalization to this constellation. . . . There occurs a process of religious inoculation by which small doses of Christianized concepts and terminology are injected into consciousness. By the time the process is completed, the individual is effectively immunized against any real encounter with the Christian message."[32]

Donald Miller suggests a fourfold educational methodology to meet this challenge. Some of this was/is non-self-consciously done by black churches in the rapprochement between the Black Revolution and Black Theology, namely, (1) develop in persons, through their ongoing involvement in a social justice praxis, an awareness of the radical social mission of the biblical message by indicating both its positive and negative responses in past/present history; (2) develop in persons, through their ongoing involvement in social justice praxis, a sense of hope and expectancy that "God confronts us in the present as One who shall fulfill in the future what he has promised and begun to establish in the past";[33] (3) provide for persons, through their ongoing involvement in social justice praxis learning situations, "contrast experiences" or encounter experiences with injustice in other forms and contexts and/or "contrast experiences" in their own context; and (4) develop in persons, in and through their ongoing involvement in a social justice praxis, a sense of community and a quality of commitment that will call them to and sustain them in social change roles and ministries.

Characteristic V: Programmatic Integration

Black churches or congregations, generally, historically, and presently but more particularly since the Black Revolution in the late 1960s, have viewed themselves as having varying degrees of accountability not only to their local church families, their constituents, and their denominations but also to the black communities in which they are located. Further, this relationship to the community has usually been one of humane concern for the general health and welfare of its children, youth, and adults and for its family, economic, social, and political life as well. This has resulted in a communal-type experience of church relationship style that has allowed the black church to view its ministry holistically, both locally and in a community sense. This perspective has meant that the black church tends to consider the whole person in all of his/her varied relationships as the necessary and proper focus of ministry.

Social justice ministries in the black church, then tend to be congregation-oriented rather than committee-oriented, and mission-directed rather than externally influenced.

By contrast, many nonethnic constituency churches tend to make or draw distinctions between personal and social aspects of the gospel, private and public witness to its teachings, and individual rather than corporate responses to the challenges of the collective issues of the public domain. Dieter Hessel firmly believes that a strategy for a social justice ministry in congregations like these should be a broad and pervasive qualitative endeavor that includes the whole gamut of the life of the church: individual and corporate; cross-model, for example, social justice ministries and liturgy; interdisciplinary, for example, biblical-ethical; contextual or focused through congregational issues; missional and integrated.[34]

A Basic Framework

The following proposal for a framework for a model of religious education from the perspective of the black religious experience is part of an essay entitled "Black Theology and Religious Education," published in Randolph Crump Miller, ed., *Theology of Religious Education* (Birmingham: Religious Education Press, 1995), pages 321-22 and 324-35. The theological sources for the model in this essay may be found in the previous section. Shockley now makes the case for a black perspective on Christian religious education, takes note for the first time in a published work of strategies indigenous to black churches, and further refines the trajectory of his own thinking toward a religious education that would draw its inspiration from the creative engagement by black churches with a theological and cultural heritage originating in Africa and negotiated through their encounters with the religious education traditions of white churches.

New Black Church Paradigm

The black church that emerged from the black revolution of the late 1960s was a surprisingly timely response to the pre-black revolution traditional black church. It was not only a response to the triumphant cry for identity, equality, and self-determination, it was a viable alternative to white Christianity and white American theology constructs which historically had held that black religion, generally, was "defective." Additionally, it was a response to either the unwillingness or the inability of white North American Christianity to offer more than rhetoric to the challenge of inclusiveness, white ethnocentrism, and racism.

What was the outline of the new Black Church Paradigm claiming a holistic approach to a ministry with the oppressed? Gayraud Wilmore identified four axioms of an autonomous, free-standing system. He emphasized:

1. The renewal and enhancement of the black church in terms of its liturgical life, its theological interpretation [and], its understanding of its mission. . . .
2. The development of the black church, not only as a religious fellowship, but as a community of organization . . . which uses its resources . . . the black community.
3. The projection of a new quality of church life which would equip and strengthen the church as custodian and interpreter of that cultural heritage which is rooted and in the peculiar experience of black people . . . and the faith that has sustained them.
4. The contribution of the black church, out of its experience of suffering and the yearning for freedom, of that quality of faith, hope, and love which can activate, empower, renew, and unite the whole church of Christ.[35]

This "paradigm shift, embodying a new set of conceptual, methodological, and theoretical assumptions,"[36] significantly reoriented the black church and gave it a widely acclaimed self-authenticating mandate to "do" ministry contextually, that is, in distinctive and unique ways. This "praxis" move by an appreciable number of black churches was not precipitous. It was made with the full realization that it would alienate many nonradicalized black clergy and laypersons as well as many so-called liberal whites in biracial denominations. It was made because a majority of forward-thinking black church leaders knew, in Gayraud Wilmore's words, that "it may be the last opportunity for the church to break out of its symbolic commitment to the illusionary goal of one-way integration and permeate the black community with a positive concept of power and sense of transcendent vocation that will serve the purposes, justice, and freedom."[37]

The Search for Models

The search for models that embody the radical visioning, commitment, awareness, reflection, and intentionality that are necessary for the development of a black theology-inspired educational approach was difficult.

The result is a composite of concepts, constructs, experimental programs, and theories, which have addressed education for liberation in culturally diverse communities by black and white educationists and religious educators.

It is now our task to interrelate these various fragments into an ethno-cultural black church education-for-liberation-paradigm for predominantly, but not exclusively, black congregations.

Underlying Assumption

Undergirding the design that is being presented is the assumption that a crucial and definitive aspect of the nature and purpose of the church is to be revolutionizing as well as a reconciling presence in the personal, social, and world-life of the church. The new situation in the church and in society requires a critical theological and educational analysis such as black theology has suggested. Again, congregations must be radicalized over the issues of racism and national, economic, and social development. Robert McAfee Brown suggests that "we are called upon to develop a theology of the world, more than a theology of the church; or if it is to be a theology for the church, it must be a theology for the church-that-exists-not-for-itself-but-for-the sake-of-the-world."[38]

Transformative Education

A complementary educational philosophy for black theology could well be Paulo Freire's "transformational learning." Resting firmly on a humanist belief that education should be an instrument of liberation for the oppressed and the oppressor, Freire insists that both the oppressed and the oppressor "name" their world. This is basic for authentic humanity. With this new power to name their world they may also discern previously unrealized options and voluntarily pursue courses of action to obtain and maintain their freedom. The method by which this can be accomplished involves four steps: (1) an acute sense of awareness of one's oppression and oppressors; (2) a realistic analysis of the extent and impact of the "limit situations" imposed and the "limit acts" required for liberation; (3) an articulation of the critical action or praxis that must follow analysis if education is to be more than intellectual emptiness; and (4) verification or ascertaining that the "new" person born in this process is "no longer oppressor or oppressed, but . . . in the process of achieving freedom."[39]

HOLISTIC CHURCH EDUCATION

Black church education for liberation suggests the need for a holistic approach, that is, an approach concerned with the entire system in question. Dieter Hessel's holistic or integrated model for implementing the liberation education program is well-suited to do this. Applied to black churches interested in a liberation model of education it would have several implications.

First, it would be in basic agreement with Susan Thistlethwaite that justice (in this case liberation) must become an identity for the churches desiring such a ministry and not just a panel of issues.[40] Second, as Hessel suggests, each ministry of the church, for example, preaching, teaching, and worship, should have some "liberation education" character. Third, in implementing Hessel's approach the lectionary for the Christian year would be used (see Hessel's *Social Themes of the Church Year*). This ecumenical commentary on the lectionary of the Christian year explores potential uses and meanings for teaching about social justice issues on an annual basis.

There are five foundations for Hessel's holistic approach: (1) critical reflection on ministry including linkage "between worship, teaching, and public engagement"; (2) scriptural grounding "in the biblical story of the social God" who "creates us with promise, commissions us by grace, and sends us into mission"; (3) an insistence that no distinction be made between the personal and social aspects for the Christian faith; (4) faithfulness to the gospel involving "public engagement simultaneously with personal integration"; and (5) participation in the life of the "church redemptive" as the singular authentic center of "God's transforming activity."[41]

TEACHING AND LEARNING FOR DISCIPLESHIP

Sara Little's "discipleship model" offers interesting insights for black liberation theology and the teaching-learning process. It does so, however, by raising a difficult question. She asks, "How does one include actual acts of effecting social justice as teaching?" She goes on to question whether just "doing" is "doing the truth" to use a phrase of Thomas Groome. Little believes that "simulating," "planning," and "contriving" experiences is not too meaningful. She is convinced that it is important

114

to work with persons and situations "to help—[them] relate the gospel to their situation, learning with them and working to move toward 'responsible freedom.'" Her process for achieving this is a four-phase one: Awareness; Analysis; Action; Reflection.

Awareness: A learning process phase designed to increase levels of awareness and understanding in reference to "God's intention and purpose for human life" and "the Christian's responsibility to be involved."

Analysis: A learning process phase in which information and facts are gathered, explored, and perceived in relation to goals, resources, alternatives, urgency, and the integrity of the gospel.

Action: A learning process phase in which participating individual, personal, and/or corporate action "consistent with the Christian ethic" and directed toward the establishment of social justice (liberation) is enacted.

Reflection: A learning process phase in which planned-for theological reflection on the praxis experience is held "to test the ethical assumption of our perception of God's will on which the action was based."[42]

RELATIONAL TEACHING FOR PEACE AND JUSTICE

Working from within a somewhat different educational construct, James McGinnis projects a "relational" model, that is, one that "moves from awareness to concern to action" in a program "to educate for peace and justice." Premised on the belief that peace (and other social justice concerns) is not simply a concept to be taught, but a reality to be lived, awareness, concern, and action are deployed as the basis for conscientious decision making in the following ways:

Awareness of social justice issues and the disposition to work for change would be encouraged by "promoting a sense of self-esteem" and a feeling that our "gifts" should be shared with others for the good of all.

Concern about social issues is to be nurtured into a sense of solidarity with the victims of injustices. Such a link is crucial for action.

Action itself should eventuate from concern. It may take the form of direct service, acting on local issues, and/or action within one's "Zones of freedom."[43]

TEACHING FOR SYSTEMIC CHANGE

A final allied approach to liberation education with black theology as a base could be Suzanne Toten's System Change Model.[44]

In a courageous attempt to confront and answer the question, "What would it mean to respond seriously to the turmoil and suffering of our world," Suzanne Toten is convinced that religious education must go beyond the domestic issues of church education and even beyond "consciousness raising" and "value change" learning. Her insightful thesis is "that if justice is to be central to religious education, it must play a role in effecting structural and systemic change." More explicitly, educational efforts to change individual attitudes and value systems must be realistically viewed in relation to "the nature of social structures and the web of structural relationships that make up the social order." In her food crisis research, for an example, she found that national policy and legislation on this issue "is structured primarily to meet the economic interests of our country and only secondarily to meet the needs of hungry people." Implicit in this critique is a basic issue for religious education in reference to social justice. Can structures and systems be placed beyond criticism and succumbed to as a patriotic duty? Further, can Christians do this?

Toten offers several suggestions toward engaging the problem of the system nature of injustice. Commencing with a distinction between religious and general or public education she asserts that the peculiar task of religious education regarding injustice is to stand with them "to create a world of justice, peace, and love [and] to remove whatever breeds oppression, be it personal, structural, or systemic."

Toward a New Paradigm

This closing section of the chapter dealing with black theology and religious education will cite four black church liberation education models sympathetic to if not oriented in black theology assumptions. At the conclusion of these model-presentations a black church education-for-liberation paradigm will be suggested. Including segments and insights from non-black as well as black religious educators, it will reflect an ethnocultural approach to the theory and practice of religious education in black churches. But first a critique of the models just discussed.

Critique of White Churches

In black perspective, the models for social justice ministries previously discussed need to be critiqued. Essentially, while helpful, suggestive, and even provocative, they yield less than adequate solutions to the problems faced by black churches committed to black theology: Several things may account for this:

First, social justice and especially black liberation ministries are rarely, if ever, central in mission, ministry, or program in non-black churches. This being the case they are routinely marginalized and low-prioritized. Peter Berger is perhaps correct when in referring to white Christianity he says, religion is "functional" rather than "dysfunctional" in reference to the status quo. It tends to provide the "integrating" symbols rather than the "symbols of revolution."[45]

Second, there is little hard evidence to believe that racial majority churches are ready, willing, or able to go beyond their customary "ministries of intervention" and seriously challenge the violent and persistent structures and systems that are the root causes of injustice, oppression, and racism and that cause the underclasses to suffer.

Third, the churches of the oppressors do not deal on a face-to-face or day-to-day basis with the oppressed. Their contact is impersonal and buffered. Further, their institutions, especially their churches, are usually safely distanced from the consequences of their behavior or policies.

For these and similar reasons black theology has found it almost universally necessary to create and develop support systems and strategies for liberation ministries outside of white colleague-churches.

Black Church Liberation Education Models

Since the black revolution of the late 1960s several black religious educators have advanced church/congregational models for church education. One of the earliest of these had been projected by Yvonne Delk (United Church of Christ) in the late 1960s. The rationale for coming forth with this model was Delk's sense of the need to confront the lack of identity, self-worth, and self-esteem in black children, youth, and adults. From her point of view a four-point program of religious education was needed to correct these omissions: (1) the rehearsal of the story of "who we are" through study-reflection-action modules based on African and

117

African-American history and religious faith; (2) a recovery of the positive values of learning reflected in the African oral tradition; (3) the reexploration of the values in intergenerational learning and teaching in black churches; and (4) serious, personalized, and relevant Bible study as a grounding for religious education. Strategic themes for this biblical curriculum are "hearing the word;" "interpreting the word;" "living the word;" and "acting the word."[46]

Saturday Ethnic School Model

Concurrently with the work of Yvonne Delk was the contribution of Olivia Stokes, the first black person to be appointed to the professional staff of the National Council of Church's Division of Christian Education. Through the "Black Christian Education Project" Stokes assisted in setting the direction of religious education for a decade with the following definition of the task of religious education in the black church. Consonant with the substance of the black theology statements of the time she said in essence that the task was to join theological reflection with those processes which expose the structures which enslave, to develop techniques for freedom, and give structure to those values of the black experience for building community for God's people.[47]

Stokes was also largely responsible for initiating and implementing the Saturday Ethnic School model. The following are its objectives:

- To develop a curriculum emphasizing black church history, black history, and contemporary issues.
- To develop creativity within its members enabling them to express their religious feelings through drama, music, painting, poetry, and creative writing.
- To provide a forum for youth and adult expression of the need for community development, social and political solidarity, and other liberation issues.
- To provide a Black Resource Center for the black community. In such a center African and African American culture and heritage would be studied and taught, greatly enhancing the self-esteem and self-development of African American students and others.

118

Oral Tradition Model

Based on several years of study, teaching, research, and travel in Africa, especially West Africa, Ella Mitchell[48] developed a contextual education model for religious education in the black church. For Mitchell "contextual" means the structuring, guidance, and interpretation of what goes on in the home, community, and society as a matter of course. In her words, "Both words and living examples are effective, whether formally or informally given, because they occur in the midst of a related experience." Several insights came out of Mitchell's work both here in the United States and in Africa.

1. The basic pattern of oral communication and learning are rooted in African rather than African American culture.
2. Many "so-called" illiterate cultures communicate their religious beliefs more effectively than some "so-called" literate ones.
3. The oral process of learning is a legitimate system of teaching and retention. Its methodology should and could be extrapolated into African American educational experience.
4. Early African and early African American teaching and learning was "contextual," that is, carried on in relation to ongoing life experiences.
5. Contextual/oral tradition learning data and methods included: slave cabin life; slave field conversation; mealtime table talk; the secret "church" meeting; plantation churches; storytelling, music, dancing, and proverbial sayings.

African American Model

Joseph Crockett, Director of United Methodist Racial and Ethnic congregations before assuming a teaching position at Colgate Rochester Divinity School, raised a number of questions about teaching/learning scripture among African Americans. What influences their learning? How is scripture taught? What is the role and function of cultural heritage in church education?

These questions and further issues of content and interpretation lie behind his development of an African American teaching-learning model.

Three general principles govern this effort toward multicultural curriculum design:

- The inseparability but distinguishability between African American sources of religious experience.
- The necessity of approaching the interpretation task with openness rather than preconcluded views.
- The "weighing of scripture in relation to African Americans' personal and communal feelings, thoughts, and life tasks."

In concluding this African American approach, four functional strategies are suggested:

- The *story* strategy integrating identity and vocation issues through storytelling,
- The *exile* strategy focusing on heritage, tradition, and God's loving care and call to Christian community,
- The *Exodus* strategy emphasizing the unique missional, justice, and social engagement responsibility of the African American Church,
- The *sanctuary* strategy acknowledging the central place of the church community in African American life, especially in its worship aspect.[49]

An Ethnocultural Black Church Education-for-Liberation Paradigm

The resultant composite ethnocultural black church education-for-liberation model will be discussed under several headings: challenge; mission; guidelines; church involvement; teaching; learning; curriculum construction; and leadership development.

CHALLENGE

The black church must set itself to deal with several major issues in this closing decade of the century. Otherwise it may not continue to command the respect and credibility of many of its followers:

It must respond more unequivocally to the continuing and desperate demands of the vast numbers of what William Julius Wilson calls "the truly disadvantaged," that is, the growing underclass, the homeless, the many new types of families, the victims of AIDS, the black poor, and others crying for assistance.[50]

Second, it must renew the waning enthusiasm for black pride, self-esteem, cultural integrity, and indigeneity. This must be done while not failing to pursue what Walter Brueggemann has so aptly called the "central vision of world history in the Bible, namely, that . . . of every creature in community with every other living in harmony and security toward the joy and well-being of every other creature."[51] Third, it must position itself to offer to black and other Christians alike a new understanding of black theology which Rosemary Ruether has called "a possible form of theology as a whole." Fourth, the churches and their people must disengage themselves from parochialism and racism and intentionally engage in the personal and social transforming ministries of the gospel that alone can reconcile all persons in Christ.

MISSION

The black church cannot assume universally that its members understand, accept, and proactively pursue a central tenet of the church universal to be a revolutionary force not only in personal lives but society as well. Many black members as well as white may not realize with Paul Lehmann that the "Christian should have known about revolution all along . . . and only the non-Christian . . . (be) surprised at revolution."[52]

GUIDELINES

Several guidelines are being suggested for black churches and other churches wishing to align black theology and religious education in the local church: "Black theology and religious education can find a common base in their common task, i.e., to respond to the call to social engagement by God who is fully social and radically present in the world."[53] Such a response "frontlines" social and political involvement and gives the church an "identity" as an advocate of liberation.

CHURCH INVOLVEMENT

If, as black theology cogently states, God acts in history to redeem the oppressed and that he has acted decisively in the Incarnation to

demonstrate this, churches must be involved in the black struggle for liberation. As the continuing presence of Christ on earth, their ministries
represent Christ and what they do represents him as well. It is reasonable,
then, to expect the church through its educational program to strive to
accomplish what Christ would accomplish, especially among the
oppressed. This holistic ministry by the whole congregation to the whole
person in his/her whole context, then, calls the church to be the "people
of God."[54] Randolph Crump Miller interprets this to mean that "one
finds . . . vocation at the centers of power, that the ministry of the laity is
crucial in terms of the religious issues in political action, economic decisions, and social concerns."[55]

TEACHING-LEARNING

The educational foundation for a black liberation-oriented religious
education is praxis-learning, that is, interactive reflection toward the
actual transformation of an actual situation. Unless this crucial motif is
in the design of the black church's ministry and intentionally pursued,
the heart of Christian teaching is being denied. Paulo Friere speaks to
this: "Within the word we find two dimensions, reflection and action in
such radical interaction that if one is sacrificed . . . the other immediately
suffers. There is no true word that is not at the same time a praxis."[56]

CURRICULUM CONSTRUCTION

There are three major objectives in constructing a curriculum and
developing curriculum resources for an ethnocultural black church education-for-liberation educational experience:

Biblical/Theological/Historical Integrity: The black religious experience is
replete with Old and New Testament references and images of God's concern for justice, righteousness, and freedom. In the life and teachings of
Jesus, examples of Jesus' concern for persons and human need abound, for
example, his solidarity with the poor, his association with the outcast,
and his identification with the "marginal" people of his day. These modules are basic for curriculum construction for all ages and groups in the
black church liberation thrust. Essential themes to be emphasized are:
God is the Lord of history; God is concerned about and involved in history; God is the God of the oppressed; and God came to liberate all
oppressed and oppressors in the historical person of Jesus Christ.

Contextual Reality: Curriculum construction must take the context
(setting) of black religious experience seriously. It should teach believing

that the activity of God primarily occurs in the midst of the trials and tribulations of the oppressed of every kind. James Cone explains this when he defines black theology as "that theology which arises out of the need to articulate the significance of black presence in a hostile white world." William Jones makes the same point when saying, "each Black Theology presents itself, implicitly or explicitly as a specific strategy for black liberation."[57]

Systemic Engagement: Biblical integrity and contextual reality lead to a third crucial foundation of the curriculum—systemic engagement. Essentially this means that students should learn to identify, analyze, correct, or eliminate restraining or destructive structures and/or systems that support and sustain oppression, racism, or sexism. This was Martin Luther King's concern. "King's perception of the human problem . . . led him to emphasize . . . that his struggle was directed against the forces, or structure of evil itself rather than against the person or group . . . doing the evil."[58]

LEADERSHIP DEVELOPMENT

Discovering, enlisting, training, and supporting teachers and leaders for an ethnocultural black church education-for-liberation program presents a unique challenge. In addition to the standard qualifications expected from those who will direct and/or lead groups, for example, visioning group goals, sensing skill limits and potential, image and self-esteem building, initiative, group participation skills, liberation oriented leaders-educators will possibly need still other abilities.

Liberation-oriented education in the local congregation will require a unique enabling style of leadership, committed to the concept of the black church as a potential agency for basic social change and to the belief that persons must and can come to a realization of the need for change. Black parents, teachers, group leaders, officials, and clergy in black churches will need immersion in and exposure to a variety of learning theories and leadership styles from which to glean and construct a personally meaningful style of leadership and learning method.

SECTION IV

To Create the Beloved Community: A *Prophetic Christian Education for the Twenty-first Century*

In this final chapter, Fred Smith, in consultation with Charles Foster, builds on the themes of Grant Shockley's work to develop a view of Christian education that draws on the resources and traditions of the black church and religious experience. In writing this chapter, Smith has had the advantage of being able to engage a range of black and womanist theologies and research into the African sources to the African American experience that simply were not available to Grant. Yet as we discovered throughout this project, Grant anticipated many of these themes. We, therefore, delight in extending the trajectory of his thought, while taking full responsibility for its final form. We offer this final chapter consequently, as an expression of our appreciation of the pioneering work of Grant Shockley. May his legacy live on!

"It is ironic and troublesome to realize that in the 1980s Christian churches in America are still so racially segregated that their religious education programs require separate-chapter treatments in the same book. Even more ironic is the fact that this is the only way that it could have been done. These programs are completely separate and this dilemma is inevitable in a de facto segregated society that allows itself to be ruled by the logic of illogical color prejudice."[1]

Grant Shockley

Introduction

Grant Shockley lived out his vocation in the United Methodist Church, an overwhelmingly white denomination that segregated the black experience within it. He received his theological education at predominantly white Drew Theological Seminary after graduating from Lincoln University, an historic black college. These three formative institutions provided a peculiar platform from which to engage the task of developing a model for Christian education that took seriously the plight of African Americans in a racist Christian society and church.

Racism and segregation were the primary issues that defined the problematic in this task for Grant.

> The deeper question for Protestantism, however, is how long does it intend to tolerate this segregated situation or how long does it think its influence can survive such segregation? Protestantism has almost completely failed in its attempt to inculcate its most essential teachings about the unity of humankind, the equality of all persons before God, and the ideal of a divinely intended community of love, justice, reconciliation, and peace.[2]

The formative events in the history of race relations for Grant Shockley took place in the 1960s and 1970s. These were the heydays of Black Theology and Black Power, the Civil Rights Movement, Latin American Liberation Theology, and the African Independence Movements. The people and events of these movements provide the historical backdrop for the articles we have reviewed and discussed in this book.

Grant's work did not take into account the fall of the Berlin wall and the end of the Cold War; his work did not witness the end of Apartheid and the Truth and Reconciliation Commission or the rapid democratization of Latin America. Grant spoke of the "Global Village" in orbit of "a single moral universe," but he could not have anticipated the advent of globalization in the orbit of a single global economy. Grant spoke of development as a new term for missions and missionary education, but he did not anticipate the role that faith-based organizations would play in the task of reconstruction and community development in an era of post civil rights and welfare reform. Grant's work was prophetic in that it foreshadowed these events but did not address them.

Grant's writings on Christian education were always prophetic in that his was a critique of the white Protestant church and of the black church in particular. As a prophet he spoke from the edges of both communities, marginalized, however, in the white world, and largely unappreciated by the black world. He resided, for the most part, in the temples of learning and denominational altars of power. Yet, his heart remained with the downtrodden masses of black people and the religion and church that sought to lift them up.

In a sense, almost ahead of his time, Grant embraced the philosophy of pluralism and sought to apply it to the black church and religious education. As an African American, however, he could not escape the dichotomy of black and white. As a Christian educator residing on the edges of both congregation and academy, he could not avoid the tensions that existed between them—tensions often greater than between black and white communities. To a predominantly white academic audience he wrote an apology for the black religious education experience, seeking to communicate on behalf of the black community the meaning and value of the black experience to the larger human ecology. To the black church he wrote an apology for Christian education and Black Theology. His early work largely comprised reciting the history and promoting the value of the black religious education experience and the role the white church played in the religious education of blacks. Later he championed the role of Black and Liberation Theologies in the Christian education of the black church. This double-edged message noted the role whites played in the development of the Christian education in the black church experience while advocating at the same time the role that the black religious education experience could play in the life of the church in general.

The African roots of the Christian religious experience for black people and the black church's own efforts in religious education—especially in small and rural congregations—with few exceptions are largely missing in his writing. His lack of attention can be attributed to an historical blindness that existed in the scholarship of most of his era. Only late in his career did the indigenous black experience from the sixteenth through the nineteenth centuries in North America catch the imagination of scholars. Given his appreciation for African culture and life, he would undoubtedly have written differently if the literature from this new research had been available. As we look at a projection of these themes in Grant's works, we must not only take into account recent scholarship in the African heritage of the black church, we must continue to look at the evolution of race relations in the academy and society. From this vantage point the question undergirding Grant's quest—"Does the church, specifically the black church, want Christian education?"—no longer dominates our attention. Instead we find ourselves asking: "Is there anything indigenous to the black experience that is not religious education?"

Answers to that question actually extend and deepen Grant's quest for a religious education that locates a primary source for social change in and through the black church. The liberative consequences of an education that produced prophets to speak to the racism and oppression of black people (and all people) also spoke prophetically to black and white institutions. Grant discovered in "an examination of the evolution of the pastoral leadership, in ethnic and black churches (in response to past, continuing, and present needs and demands for justice, equality, and liberation in the church and in the general society), a paradigm" for "an integrated social justice ministry for local congregations that is prophetic, holistic, and transformational." This insight led him to conclude, "Unless and until churches (black, white, or other) commit themselves to these elemental presuppositions, the integrity of their total design for either ministry or education must be questioned."[3]

For Grant, answers to the question of integrity could be found in the church's own history. "It is suggested" he wrote, "that the church again confront itself with the forthright, critical insights of its own neglected Reformed tradition. Among other things, this tradition emphasizes the kingdom of God as the goal of the human community and the prophetic word as the conscience of the nation."[4] One does not have to read deeply into Grant's writings to identify them as prophetic. Although Grant never mentions the term "Beloved Community," his works clearly point toward the "Kingdom of God as a human community with a prophetic word as its conscience." In this regard his views are consistent with the themes in Martin Luther King Jr.'s vision of a "Beloved Community."

Grant sought to be a prophetic voice in Christian education, and he clearly sought to develop a prophetic model for Christian education, grounded in the black religious experience, that would intentionally engage the issues that held that experience in bondage. He died before he completed that quest. The book he envisioned to draw on the new scholarship in the indigenous religious heritage of African Americans was never written. The rest of this chapter takes up that task, building on the foundation of his work, but reflecting my own understanding, as one Grant mentored, of that religious experience.

Prophetic Christian Education

But Peter, standing up with the eleven, lifted up his voice, and said unto them, "Ye men of Judea, and all ye that dwell at Jerusalem, be this known unto you, and hearken to my words: . . . This is that which was spoken by the prophet Joel; And it shall come to pass in the last days, saith God, I will pour out of my Spirit upon all flesh: and your sons and your daughters shall prophesy, and your young men shall see visions, and your old men shall dream dreams: And on my servants and on my handmaidens I will pour out in those days of my Spirit; and they shall prophesy."(Acts 2:14-18 KJV)

Sociologist Theodore E. Long[5] claims that most sociologists, following the lead of Max Weber, define the term *prophet* as one standing outside of existing structures making claims on behalf of transcendent powers. As we have seen, this certainly describes Grant Shockley's ministry. Prophetic claims challenge social authority, thereby creating opportunities for and stimulating action to transform or undermine existing regimes. From this Weberian perspective,[6] prophecy has traditionally been conceived as:

1. charismatic leadership derived from charismatic authority.
2. political response of the alienated to societal crisis arising outside of routine institutional order.
3. a revolutionary force challenging existing authority to institute major socio-political change.[7]

Long argues that sociologists have misunderstood Weber's conception of prophecy by equating it with charismatic authority and implying that prophets are marginal persons without legitimate credentials or resources, while receiving, at the same time, legitimation from others also disaffected in status quo institutions. This view of prophecy conversely implies that ordinary people from all kinds of backgrounds (including those within status quo institutions) cannot be prophets. Long reassesses Weber's conception of prophecy to mean personal charisma rather than charismatic authority. From this perspective:

1. prophecy may arise within established groups and institutions and not exclusively from among alienated and marginalized persons.

2. prophecy need not always wait for internal social crisis but instead, may arise as an expression of group solidarity.
3. prophecy is primarily a religious phenomenon, not a political one, originating in and primarily directed toward the religious life of a people.[8]

Long defines "prophecy as the charismatic proclamation/demonstration of divine claims and judgments on human life and institutions by one who feels called to that mission."[9] From this perspective the task of a prophet is to proclaim, demonstrate, or educate persons in a divine message in the hope that all human life may submit to a transcendent meaning system. Thus it follows that a task of prophetic Christian education *is to educate persons to the divine message (prophecy) of a transcendent meaning system (a sense of transcendence) in order to change oppressive structures and human life.* In Peter's Pentecost sermon, recorded in the Acts of the Apostles, we may discern many of the general characteristics of New Testament Christian prophetic religion:

1. the honoring of *charismatic personalities* and the enhancement of divine vocation (Acts 2:37, 42);
2. the upholding of a *received revelation*, the canon by which the tradition of the community is faithfully controlled (Acts 2:16, 25, 42);
3. an emphasis upon the *action* of God in Christ as the mode of revelation or metaphor of the divine message (Acts 2:22, 25, 30, 36);
4. a sense of the importance of the *cultic* aspect of religion, for example worship and praise, and the assembling of the fellowship of believers (Acts 2:41, 42, 44, 46);
5. an emphasis on *community* as necessary to the highest form of religious experience (Acts 2:44, 45, 46);
6. the drive toward *universalism* (Acts: 2:14, 21, 39, 47);
7. a demand for personal and communal *praxis* to meet the ethical demands of the received revelation of the Kingdom of God as exemplified in the life and works of Christ (Acts 2:43, 44, 45, 47).[10]

A prophetic Christian education will include many (if not all) of these features. It will be Spirit-filled and directed to the liberation, reconciliation, and transformation of the lives of people and their communities. However, Grant prophesied in very different times.

The Problematic of Double Consciousness in Prophetic Christian Education

The Negro is a sort of seventh son, born with a veil and gifted with second sight in this American world, a world which yields him no true self-consciousness, but only lets him see himself through the revelation of the other world. It is a peculiar sensation, this double-consciousness, this sense of always looking at one's self though the eyes of others, of measuring one's soul by the tape of a world that looks on in amused contempt and pity. One ever feels his twoness, —an American, a Negro; two souls, two thoughts, two unreconciled strivings; two warring ideals in one dark body, whose dogged strength alone keeps it from being torn asunder. (W. E. B. DuBois, The Souls of Black Folk)

These words of DuBois have dominated the consciousness of African American scholars for a century now. They convey a basic truth in the experience of people striving to succeed in a racist culture. Grant returned to them time and again to make sense of the black experience in the United States. African American intellectuals and professionals often feel this duality more keenly than others as they stride through both worlds. This was certainly true for Grant Shockley, but something else was also at work in his life. We would argue that his perceptions and responses to life were shaped but not dominated by double consciousness. We would further contend that his own capacity for breaking through the bonds of double consciousness may be traced to the depths of his grounding in the black religious experience. We would go on to argue that double consciousness does not dominate the personalities of others steeped in the black religious experience to the same extent that it does for those unable to enter into an authentic religious experience of the black church. Because we have a language—thanks to DuBois—to profoundly express our duality, the triune nature of our existence as participants in the black Christian religious experience often goes unexpressed and unexplained. As a Christian educator, Shockley intuited that the black religious experience had something to offer America and the world beyond its brokenness. Shockley's work seeks to help us understand what DuBois did not. The source of the "dogged strength" of which DuBois speaks is the black religious experience.

131

And yet, Grant's response to white racism was typical of that of intellectuals at the time. Trained to use the tools of an American/European academic education, he wrote from this vantage point. His writing can best be understood in the context of DuBois's notion of double consciousness—of being torn between two worlds never completely at home in either. Although he had the intellectual capacity and training to participate fully in the academic discourse of the white world, he remained conscious of being black and committed to the uplifting of the black community.

For Grant, DuBois's conception of "double-consciousness" was the black experience.

> This . . . is the life and world of any and all people of color who must or will identify themselves as being of African descent. It is the ever-present reality of knowing and feeling and living as a non-white in a white-oriented and white-controlled society. It is the Black group experience, historic and present, of being oppressed, disdained, deprived, excluded, alienated, neglected and rejected.[11]

In this and similar statements, I would contend, Grant relied too heavily on DuBois's interpretation of the duality of black consciousness to discover in his own experience a third source of human consciousness perhaps best described by William James.

DuBois's notion of double consciousness was undoubtedly inspired by James's concept of the "divided-self" of the "sick soul" in his classic *Varieties of Religious Experience*.[12] DuBois took this religious notion and made it into a sociological construct. The move we will make is more in line with what James had in mind—that is from double consciousness (as in the African and American divided self) to a reunited third consciousness (as in an African and American to a Christian/African/American sense of self). It is a journey from liberation to reconciliation to transformation. It is the journey from slave for life, to freed person, to child of God. It is the move from accommodation (mere survival), to liberation (freedom from oppression), to reconciliation (true community) resulting from a transformation of community and persons (selves). The task of a prophetic Christian education from this perspective involves the reconstruction of the black community and the reconciliation of black and white and all other communities to God in a Beloved Community.

Sources of a Prophetic Christian Education: Prophetic Christianity, Ubuntu Theology, and the Beloved Community

This view of prophetic Christian education draws on three primary sources. The first is prophetic Christianity with its emphasis on the dialectical conception of human nature and human history through which we name the reality of our experience, discover something powerful enough to hope for, and discern how to act. By attending to the tension of faith and racism with their sources in human nature, the tension of living with white domination as the reality of experience and the kingdom of God as the source of things hoped for, prophetic Christianity holds up a vision of the Beloved Community that overcomes white racism of every kind and seeks the liberation of all people.

For Cornel West, prophetic Christianity rests on two norms. One is existential—emphasizing individuality—and the other social—emphasizing democracy.[13] In the first norm the self-realization of *individuality* occurs within community. It can be understood both as penultimate social, political, economic liberation and otherworldly salvation. The second norm, *democracy* requires the accountability of institutions to the populace. A prophetic Christian education promotes as an ethical norm the notion of individuality because it emphasizes the "importance of community, common good and the harmonious development of personality." At the same time a prophetic Christian education opposes a doctrine of individualism that "promotes human self centeredness, denigrates the idea of community and distorts the holistic development of personality." West clarifies the difference. "The norm of individuality conceives persons as enjoyers and agents of their uniquely human capacities, whereas doctrinaire individualism views them as maximizers of pleasure and appropriators of unlimited resources."[14] A prophetic Christian education however, moves beyond West's notions of individuality to emphasize that people are also created in the image of God and capable of selfless acts of love.

This brings us to a second source for our understanding of individuality in a prophetic Christian education—the theology of *ubuntu*. According to Archbishop Tutu, an individual is an individual through other individuals.

We say, "a person is a person through other persons." It is not "I think therefore I am. It says rather: "I am human because I belong, I participate, I share." A person with ubuntu is open and available to others, does not feel threatened that others are able and good, for he or she has a proper self-assurance that comes from knowing that he or she belongs in the greater whole and is diminished when others are humiliated or diminished, when others are tortured or oppressed, or treated as they were less than who they are.[15]

In *ubuntu* notions of the relation of the individual and community, we can begin to discover deeper possibilities in West's norm of democracy for a prophetic Christian education. In the course of history democracies have proved they can be just as dominating, oppressive, and violent as any totalitarian regime under the influence of racism. American slavery and Jim Crow Segregation were not only tolerated under democracy but also defended on the basis of such democratic principles as states rights and property rights. John Adams, our second president, made the point nearly two centuries ago that "we have no government armed with power which is capable of contending with human passions unbridled by morality and religion." He then concluded, "Our Constitution was made only for a moral and religious people. It is wholly inadequate to the government of any other."[16] Institutions controlled by a people without religious sensibilities are no better than any other form of government. The experience of African Americans in America is evidence of John Adams's worst fears.

If West's norm of *individuality*, as refined by *ubuntu* theology, refers to the proposition that each person is equally favored by God as a divine gift of grace, then *democracy* must be understood theologically as the historical preconditions for the Beloved Community. According to the philosopher, Josiah Royce: the Beloved Community is where love and justice rule in a community of unique distinct individuals who are loved for who they are in a plurality of circumstances.[17]

This brings us to the third and primary source of a prophetic Christian education—the Beloved Community—a vision of *theo-democracy* rooted in the images of the kingdom of God found in the Scriptures. In the Beloved Community, the people who control institutions are themselves controlled by an Unseen Transcendent God, who is Love (1 John 4:8*b*).

The prophetic Christian gospel is the primary source of prophetic Christian education. It promotes a transcendent view of self that values the needs for decision making and engagement in the struggle for freedom directed to the transformation of what is in the light of what is yet-to-be. From this perspective the educational praxis of a prophetic Christian seeks existential liberation, social reconciliation, and spiritual transformation. We turn now to an exploration of the view of the self in prophetic Christian education and then to an explication of the function and methodology of a prophetic Christian education in the formation of this view.

The Self in Prophetic Christian Education

Although implicit as goal and value throughout Grant's writings, he never fully made the strategic move from liberation to reconciliation in his understanding of a prophetic Christian education. This may be traced to his reliance on DuBois for his views of the self in the African American experience. We find no reference in Grant's work to the influence of William James on the view of self that is found in DuBois's notion of "double-consciousness." James, however, had been a primary teacher and mentor of DuBois, and in James's view of the self, we find the roots of meaning DuBois found in the African American experience of double consciousness.

DuBois's *Souls of Black Folk* was written about the time William James published *The Variety of Religious Experience*. In this classic essay James describes the self as a function of consciousness involving one's relationship to one's internal, external, and transcendent environments. According to James, consciousness serves as a knowing function. It brings us in relationship to a world of pure experience by organizing it into distinct but related categories (for example, physical, spiritual, and psychosocial), which make up our particular experience of the world. Romney Moseley, following James's discussion on the functional nature of consciousness, suggests that consciousness is somehow guided by a desire that provides insight that becomes lived experience. In "Conversion: Healthy Religion and Public Life," Moseley argued that "through consciousness we are brought into contact with the immediate 'flux of life.' Within this flux, consciousness focuses our attention on what evokes our interests and satisfies our needs. Conversely, consciousness expands the scope of our experience."[18] This "flux of life" is what James calls "pure experience." Pure experience, for James, is the primal stuff of which everything is made. It consists of activity that has not been related or experience that has not been reflected upon.

For James the self comprises what he called the material, social, and spiritual self. Each contributes to the functions of consciousness. Don

Browning in *Pluralism and Personality* summarizes James's view of the self. The self is not just something on the inside of the body, but a "phenomenon stretched out upon the world, an object in the world right along with other objects, but one towards which we feel a special 'warmth' and 'intimacy.'"[19]

The material or physical self consists of all those material objects that belong to us: our property, family, the product of our hands, and the parts of our body. Browning observed that for James, the material self is more than "the immediate way these objects give us pleasure or meet our needs." We experience in their loss "a sense of 'shrinkage' of our personality, a partial conversion of ourselves to nothingness, which is a psychological phenomenon by itself."[20] Thus any denial or threat to one's property, family, or the products of one's own hands or body diminishes the self.

The social or psychosocial self internalizes the ways others view us. We have as many social selves as we have social relationships, some more important and more dominant than others. These selves can be in harmony while playing different roles, as sort of a division of labor fitting together with only a minimum of tension. They can also be in discord with one another, causing what Erikson calls "identity confusion." But to James, "one of the very strongest forces in life" is one's "image in the eyes" of the "set," a reference group a person esteems most highly.

The spiritual self is the active element of consciousness. The spiritual self is the "self of all other selves."[21] It argues over and discriminates among our moral sensibilities, conscience, and will. The spiritual self goes out and meets the incoming experience and either welcomes it or rejects it. It focuses attention and effort in a definite direction and toward a specific aim. It overcomes or succumbs to resistances to it aims. But what if the spiritual self does not have one aim but two aims that contradict each other?

Within this Jamesian view of the self, W. E. B. DuBois speaks of the spiritual striving of black consciousness in a distinctive way. In *The Souls of Black Folk* he characterizes the self as a "peculiar sensation":

> It is a peculiar sensation, this double-consciousness, this sense of always looking at one's self through the eyes of others, of measuring one's soul by the tape of a world that looks on in amused contempt and pity. One ever feels his twoness—an American, a Negro; two souls, two thoughts, two unreconciled strivings; two warring ideals in one dark body, whose dogged strength alone keeps it from being torn asunder.[22]

This "peculiar sensation" is a way of knowing and seeing as if from behind a veil. If consciousness functions to make us conscious of our place in relation to the world, double consciousness bifurcates our world and ourselves. This bifurcation leads DuBois to conclude that what he calls "double-consciousness" is one of the primary impediments to the black moral agency in the "kingdom of culture." Double consciousness describes a social self formed in a racist society burdened by white domination.

The bifurcation of environment and self through double consciousness weakens or even paralyzes Black people's moral action in the world by confusing their identities. DuBois's description of the post-Emancipation Negro points to the contradiction of double aims.

> Here in America, in the few days since Emancipation, the Black man's turning hither and thither in hesitant and doubtful striving has often made his very strength lose effectiveness, to seem like absence of power, like weakness. And yet it is not weakness,—it is the contradiction of double aims.[23]

Double consciousness robs its victims of the capacity of effective moral action in the world through double aims. These double aims cause, "two unreconciled strivings; two warring ideals in one dark body." As long as this warring goes on in the self, the self is not capable of becoming "a co-worker in the kingdom of culture" or the kingdom of God. DuBois sees in "double-consciousness" a reference to a spiritual self whose identity or social self is confounded by social conditions that cause one to waver between conflicting and contradictory aims.

The environment that shapes the identity for the oppressed includes one's own culture (one's reference group), the oppressor's culture (the dominant group), and the culture of oppression encompassing both, which constructs the hierarchy of their relationships. In this pathogenic framework the relationship of self and environment creates a facade that prevents both the oppressed and the oppressor from seeing how their environment dehumanizes them. This is especially problematic for the oppressed who experience the environment or material self as oppressive.

In an article entitled "The Triple Quandary and the Schooling of Afro-American children," Wade Boykin characterizes the conflicting voices from three cultures that bombard the emerging sense of the social self. The noise experienced in the combination of "mainstream, oppressed minority and Black" cultures places them in a triple quandary. These African Americans are "incompletely socialized to the Euro-American

137

cultural system; they are victimized by racial and economic oppression and they participate in a culture that is sharply at odds with the mainstream ideology."[24] However, the conflicting messages among these three realms are not a struggle among equals. The mainstream Euro-American culture has a louder voice and thus it has a "hegemonic" relationship to the others.

Boykin relies on Michael Apple's description of hegemony as "an organized assemblage of meanings and practices, the central effective and dominant system of meaning, values and actions which are lived." Hegemony "leads to and comes from unequal economic and cultural control."[25] Moreover, this hegemony constitutes one's understanding of the world and sense of reality. It becomes like the air we breath or background noise.

According to Boykin, hegemony provides little difficulty for people in those minority groups who, over time, have assimilated successfully into the dominant Euro-American culture. Race however, has been the hegemonic marker blocking the assimilation of African Americans and some other minority groups into that culture. In this situation material survival has required a strong African American culture. The result is that in their early years, young African Americans are incorporated into a black cultural style—overtly and covertly—by parents and community through the deep structures of cultural patterning. At the same time, in schools dominated by Euro-American culture and practices, African American children are simultaneously re-socialized into cultural patterns that often demean and typically negate the values, perspectives, and practices learned from their black cultural experience. In this dual process of identity formation, African American children become painfully aware of their stature as members of an oppressed minority group and of the limits of the benefits of this new socialization. These are the dynamics of double consciousness in the formation of the self for today's African American youth.

Thus, an African American spiritual self is a self of an oppressed minority who must develop coping strategies within this triple quandary of negotiating with the mainstream and black cultures. The child must become a social self in the midst of these conflicts. How is this child to interpret the action of the school? What is the community of other selves that will give shape to the child's identity? To which community will the child feel accountable as he or she responds to the forces of racism? The answers to these probing questions are significant, for this triple quandary

renders life incomprehensible, unmanageable, meaningless, and ultimately incoherent.

The hegemony of the mainstream European-American culture that
sustains the status of some as an oppressed minority has made it difficult
for the African American child to become both a responsible and authentic social self. The oppositional nature of the socializing forces acting on
African American children forces them to choose one culture and negate
the other. Erik Erikson's notion of "negative identity" illumines the
effects of this struggle in the development of African American children
caught in this bind.

> The individual belonging to an oppressed and exploited minority,
> which is aware of the dominant cultural ideals but prevented from emu-
> lating them, is apt to fuse the negative images held up to him by the
> dominant majority with negative identity cultivated in his own group.
> Here we may think of the many nuances of the way in which one Negro
> may address another as "nigger".[26]

The child's historical status as an oppressed minority has made it necessary for the child to develop a spiritual self using coping strategies that
cloud the past, encapsulate the present, and limit future choices. These
coping strategies of the spiritual self often lead to dropping out of school,
drug use, violence, and teen promiscuity.

Within this Jamesian framework, Grant argued that the role of the
black church was to develop among black Christians and in the black
community a spiritual self other than that of an oppressed minority to
negotiate the twoness of the social self and to liberate the material self
from economic and political bondage. He noted:

> The Black church became the first institution in the Black community
> that dealt seriously with the split identity crisis of the comprehensive
> black-white dichotomy in North America. The significance of this fact
> cannot be underestimated for Christian education. The Black preacher
> and the Black church were of inestimable aid to Black people in nego-
> tiating the identity crisis of their "twoness" by providing in the churches
> the kind of preaching, worship, activities and programs which supported
> their groping efforts to affirm their identities, worth and aspirations as
> human beings and as children of God.[27]

In fact this third identity as "children of God" becomes a third consciousness, that while not well articulated, is implied in Grant's vision for
a Christian education grounded in the black religious experience. With

139

the consciousness of being "a child of God," the spiritual self transcends and transforms the material self burdened by racism and white domination and the social self divided by double consciousness. A prophetic Christian education, in other words, addresses the need to develop all three modes of consciousness—a sense of the material self by working toward liberation, the social self by working for reconciliation, and the spiritual self by working for transformation.

The implications of this insight are significant. Liberation in and of itself cannot solve the problem of the twoness of double consciousness. This may be most evident in the inability of the Civil Rights Movement and Black Theology to achieve their goal of eliminating racial oppression through liberation strategies. Black communities are more divided, poorer, and more segregated than before. Only a prophetic education that builds on the liberative work of the Civil Rights Movement and Black Theology into an education for reconciliation can achieve its *telos* as the kingdom of God. In the educational quest for the Beloved Community, the black church can address the needs of the material, social, and spiritual selves in a community with a universal love ethic directed toward the transformation of relationships across racial, social, economic, and gendered lines. Hence a Christian education can only be called prophetic when it embraces liberation, reconciliation, and transformation.

The Function of a Prophetic Christian Education

This chapter seeks to develop a framework for a religious education model that reflects and builds on the foundation of Grant Shockley. We argue that Grant's work provides a foundation for developing a view of prophetic Christian education as a transformational praxis to create citizens for the "Beloved Community." The function of a prophetic Christian education consequently is to create a sense of coherence in an incoherent world by developing in persons the capacities for liberation from oppression (what James called the material self), reconciliation with God and the human family (the social self), and participation with God in the transformation of the world (the praxis of the spiritual self) toward the kingdom of God in human communities imbued with the prophetic word of Love as their conscience.

The sources for a prophetic Christian education originate in a prophetic Christianity.[28] In Cornel West's understanding of prophetic Christianity we may find a way through Grant's struggle to address the peculiar sensation at the heart of human nature for blacks in America—the depravity of double consciousness. For West, human history holds human dignity and human depravity in a dialectical tension. Building on this distinction, human depravity exists in the human proclivity to cling to the moment, to refuse to transform and be transformed due to an *incoherent self*. Human dignity, by way of contrast, is found in the human capacity to contradict what is, to change and be changed, and to act in light of that which is not-yet in a struggle for a *sense of coherence*. Human dignity is the chief characteristic of what I have been calling a transcendent self.

In prophetic Christianity for West, human depravity is countered by human dignity. In this dialectical tension prophetic Christianity embodies a realistic picture of human experience. In the course of human history life is tragic and problematic; our achievements and accomplishments can never be ultimate or permanent, only relative and incoherent. And yet, countering the hold that this realistic assessment of human experience has on the human imagination, dignity is a catalyst to the coherence found in the reign of God as the possibilities of the not-yet for the hope that infuses life with meaning and purpose.

As historical creatures we live in and through the struggle between human dignity and human depravity. When human depravity prevails we become victims or objects of history—evidenced by our lack of struggle— the ultimate experience of incoherence. Through human dignity, by way of contrast, we struggle *heroically*[29] against the consequences of human depravity towards coherence. We become heroic in an historical praxis of transformation and thereby become aggressive historical antagonists against incoherence. Human history is tragic because the praxis of dignified persons (heroes and heroines) for penultimate liberation inevitably faces the limits of history and human imperfection as the negation of that same transforming praxis.

Grant located the struggle between "dignity and depravity" for African Americans in their experience of racial oppression. He also viewed the quest for human dignity that creates coherence as inherently educational. Although he never consciously identified himself as such, he took up the responsibilities of being an educational historian to chronicle the drama of black church Christian education in the quest for human dignity in the midst of human bondage.

Implicit in that drama are three themes described by West as integral to prophetic Christianity and thereby integral in a prophetic Christian education.

141

1. The *sobriety of tragedy* (historical or Christian realism), the acknowl-
   edgment of the limits of history. It is the realization that all achievements and accomplishments are relative due to the limiting and
   seemingly cyclical nature of historical time and the imperfect nature
   of human beings as agents of change.
2. The *struggle for freedom*, for an ultimate liberation. To struggle is to
   become tragic subjects of history rather than pitiful objects of history.
   To struggle for freedom means to refuse to remain a victim of pervasive victimization. To refuse without struggle is to allow others to
   determine one's future. The struggle is against historical limits that
   prevent any ultimate victory for anyone.
3. The *spirit to hope* for transhistorical salvation that makes the historical struggle not only possible but worth the trouble. The spirit of
   hope is the ever-present possibility of transcending historical limitations by pushing those limitations through struggle toward transcendence.[30]

These three themes are the integral components of the concept that I
will be calling "a sense of transcendence" found in the transformed spiritual self. The development of a transcendent self, I will argue, is the
moral, spiritual, and religious goal of a prophetic Christian education.
Guided by this goal the spiritual self may intentionally engage the conditions of oppression through the liberation of the material self, the reconciliation of the divided self, and the creation of the Beloved Community
that occurs with the transformation of the self.

These three themes form the curricular core in prophetic Christian
education. First, attention to the *sobriety of tragedy* creates the conditions
for an historical or Christian realism. It addresses the need for *critical
reflection* on the reality of human experience that allows Christians—
black and white—to speak their truth to power. Prophetic Christian education acknowledges that ultimate liberation only comes by the hands of
God. It acknowledges the humanity of both oppressed and oppressors and
refuses to take sides. A prophetic Christian educator understands that
human dignity and human depravity come in all colors. People are not to
be judged by the color of their skin, but by their willingness to be transformed and to participate in the transformation of the world according to
the prophetic Word of God. A prophetic Christian education teaches
that our freedom and liberation is not enough. No human is free until all
humankind is free.

This essential understanding of the unified self may be best expressed in the African notion of *ubuntu* introduced to us by Archbishop Desmond Tutu. In Tutu's theology of reconciliation, he has sought to restore a sense of the oppressor's humanity by releasing and enabling the oppressed to see their oppressors as peers under God. The mutuality he proposes embodies Jesus' teaching on friendship (see, for example, John 15:15). The traditional relationship of oppressor and oppressed as well as definitions of humanity based on racial classifications are shattered through *ubuntu*. *Ubuntu* is an alternative way of being in a hostile world.[31] The struggle never ceases. Our liberation is always relative. The struggle to live into the vision of the Beloved Community where the God of Love reigns consequently is both sobering and tragic.

Yet, prophetic Christian education engages teachers and learners in the *struggle for freedom* for a penultimate liberation. It seeks to equip us to become partners with God in history in the persistent and heroic struggle of people for freedom. It emphasizes action as the mode of communication of divine truth rather than words. The prophetic educator encourages persons to become agents of an historical praxis rather than its victims. Given the limits of history and human imperfection or sin, no freedom obtained in history will ever be final or ultimate. Yet, not to struggle for the freedom of self and others is to become objects of an historical process opposed to God's revealed Word for humankind. Not to struggle is to become a victim of human history and a willing participant in human depravity. This for West is really an act of cowardice. Thus a pedagogically prophetic Christian educator is a praxis educator, using action in and critical reflection on the events of our historical situation in an ongoing cycle toward transformation of self and environment in the struggle for freedom.

Finally, the *spirit to hope* for transhistorical salvation makes the historical struggle not only possible but worth the trouble. The spirit of hope resides in the prophetic Word of God communicated to humans through their visions and dreams. The spirit of hope is a dynamic force transcending history and human imperfections. It finds its power in the Holy Spirit of God that animates the Word of God in human history and through inspired human subjectivity that we experience as charisma. A gift of the Holy Spirit, charisma first of all enables one to fulfill God's purpose for the benefit of the larger community. In a prophetic Christian education charisma becomes a quality of leadership experienced as heroic. It attracts others, fosters good feeling in others, and encourages mimesis. The spirit of hope is, therefore, the charismatic and animating force of the Holy Spirit working through such leaders in the struggle for transhistorical salvation.

The implications of these three themes in a prophetic Christian education are several. Prophetic Christian education is both fully sacramental and intellectual. In this instance sacramental refers to that which attributes the efficacy of something to the mediation of the church. By intellectual I mean that which attributes its efficacy to rational arguments and proofs. In a prophetic education neither can be reduced to the other. Rather a prophetic Christian education subsumes the private and individual into an emphasis on the social and communal dimensions of human experience in its application and its impact.[32] The emphasis on *ubuntu* prevents it from taking sides with either the oppressed or the oppressors. Consequently prophetic Christian education moves beyond (not away from) Liberation and Black Theologies as it embraces *ubuntu* that is the precursor to reconciliation. A prophetic Christian education teaches values, shapes habits, and builds relationships; it nurtures and develops lived Christian faith as centered personal action in the shared quest against all forms of oppression and domination that constrain the meaning and purpose of our lives. It includes but also transcends more familiar educational emphases on cognitive structures and emotional states. The function of a prophetic Christian education, in other words, nurtures in African Americans and others a sense of transcendent selfhood that makes possible centered personal acts of liberation, reconciliation, and transformation.

A Methodology for a Prophetic Christian Education: A Prophetic Metaphorical Process: Revelation, Vision, and Praxis

Where there is no vision [prophecy] the people perish. (Proverbs 29:18a KJV)

Where there is no vision (prophecy, revelation), the people perish; they cast off restraint; they become ungovernable; they become nihilistic. Vision has to do with a sense of transcendent authority and possibilities for daily living. In the biblical tradition of Jewish and Christian commentators, vision (Hebrew *chazon*) refers to prophecy in its widest sense. It denotes the revelation of God's will as the word, or law, establishing a direction for the course of events in human history and a perspective for the actions of those in highest secular authority. Prophets instruct the people in divine things. They are religious educators—standing witnesses to the truth and power of God's word—teaching a higher than human morality.

A corresponding theme in the same biblical tradition conveys an equally powerful message. A lack of vision or apprehension of the revelation of God's will leads to confusion, disorder, rebellion, and thus incoherence. Incoherence is analogous to nihilism, which is the philosophy that regards all values as baseless and hopeless. It typifies the rejection of all natural certainty in moral values. In nihilism moral values are emptied of transcending tenets. Since they are assumed to be finite and limited, people are typically willing to refute them. To counter this possibility, Stanley Hauerwas argues that "actions must be based on our vision of what is most real and valuable" and challenges us to "discover metaphors" through which we may best see and understand our condition.[33]

Metaphors, in other words, carry prophetic visions revealing the world as seen through the eyes of God. Adapting this metaphorical viewpoint, I view vision as learning "to see" the world under the model of the divine. We seek metaphors, in other words, to help us see and understand both our condition and the divine. At least one implication is significant for this discussion. Individuals do not simply "believe" certain propositions about God; they learn to attend to reality through them. This kind of learning is transformative; it trains the whole attention (mental, affective, kinetic) and juxtaposes our experience with a divine vision of the world around us. This brings us to the heart of a prophetic Christian education. As a metaphorical praxis, prophetic Christian education helps us participate in the transformation of the world according to God's revelation. Vision as the actual contact between God and the human spirit is the necessary condition of any direct revelation. The law, the recorded result of such a revelation, is passed from mouth to mouth by tradition or written permanently in a book to serve as a guide to moral action or behavior. Indeed, where there is no living revelation, no perceived contact between humans and God, the bonds that hold society together are relaxed and broken. Through Prophetic Christian education the revelation can be presented to the human spirit (vision) in ways that shape moral behavior and action toward transforming the world (praxis).

Presenting Metaphorical Visions

The methodology of a prophetic Christian education, in this context, is to present persons with developmentally appropriate metaphors by which they may come to see and understand their condition differently. Through these metaphors persons can discern who they should be, what they can hope for, and how they ought to act. Prophetic Christian education, in other words, is a metaphorical process by which a person can see not only how they should be, but how their world should be; not just what to hope for, but how to achieve it; not just how one ought to act, but how to change action into a transforming praxis of self and the world in light of God's revealed Word.

One example of this methodology is employed in Joseph V. Crockett's *Teaching Scripture: From an African American Perspective.* Crockett develops four metaphors—Story, Exile, Sanctuary, and Exodus—as strategies for Christian education. For Crockett a metaphorical methodology allows an image to take on multiple dimensions.

> "Story" is the metaphorical reference for this strategy. The metaphor of story has at least three dimensions. One, story refers to the history of African Americans. Two, Story is used to refer to particular passages from scripture. For example, we speak of the story of creation, the story of the Exodus, the story of Jesus, the parables, and so forth. Third dimension of story emphasizes its theological aspects. It refers to the drama of God's actions in history. Jesus of Nazareth is the story's main character, and through the writing, witness, traditions, and actions of the Christian community the drama continues to unfold.[34]

This metaphorical process ties together the African American story and the biblical story. Through the drama of God's actions in history both are transcendent. The African American story of slavery, oppression, and discrimination is now placed in the context of God's unfolding drama. This perspective helps African Americans transcend the experience of double consciousness by participating in sacred history. It awakens them to a sense of transcendence that corrects their tendency to limit their attention to the dynamics of depravity rather than to sources of human dignity.

The "old folks" knew something about the possibilities for hope and transcendence in this process. They had a different point of reference outside their historical context. It enabled them to relativize the historical present. This is what I mean by transhistorical consciousness. It is as if they lived simultaneously in all times. They made bricks without straw. They crossed the Red Sea with Moses in the book of Exodus. At the same time they endured North American slavery and celebrated the Emancipation Proclamation on June nineteenth ("Juneteenth"). They suffered the indignity and poverty of a Jim Crow South and shared the Dream of Dr. Martin Luther King, Jr. The old folks hope for a "this worldly" was mingled with their hope for an "otherworldly" salvation. They lived in the spirit of hope. They knew with uncommon certainty that "trouble don't last always and were so glad that trouble don't last always."

This spirit of hope provided our elders with the sense of possibility for a transhistorical or otherworldly salvation. And that possibility made the struggle for a "this worldly" liberation not only possible but worthwhile. The religion of my grandmother and my great Auntie Lily helped them to speak of their oppression and struggle from another perspective than that held by those of us trapped inside our circumstances. They were able to achieve a "heavenly" or transcendent perspective on their circumstances. They possessed, in other words, what I have been referring to as a sense of transcendent selfhood.

The Hope-Bringer

Old Massa met our hope-bringer all right, but when Old Massa met him, he was not going by his right name. He was traveling, and touristing around on the plantations as the laugh-provoking Brer Rabbit. So Old Massa and Old Miss and their young ones laugh with and at Brer Rabbit and wished him well. And all the time, there was High John de Conquer playing his tricks of making a way out of no-way. Hitting a straight lick with a crooked stick. Winning the jack pot with no other stake but a laugh. Fighting a mighty battle without outside-showing force, and winning his war from within. Really winning in a permanent way, for he was winning with the soul of the black man whole and free. So he could use it afterwards. For what shall it profit a man if he gain the whole world and lose his soul? You would have nothing but a cruel, vengeful, grasping monster come to power.[35]

I am proposing that prophetic Christian education can also facilitate the heroic metaphorical representation of the "hope-bringer" of slave folklore for African Americans today. According to Robert Penn Warren,

"To create a hero is, indeed, to create a self."[36] Warren makes the point that the hero/heroine is not just an expression of a pre-existing self, nor only a projection of that self. Rather the hero/heroine belongs primarily to the process whereby the self emerges metaphorically. In the same way a prophetic Christian education as a metaphorical educational process for creating religious heroes and heroines can bring hope to contemporary African Americans.

The question is not whether or not African Americans will have metaphorical models (real or imagined) that will serve heroically as models of identity formation. According to John W. Roberts, professor of folklore and folklife, cultures select and promote heroes/heroines to fit their historical needs.

> The heroes that we create are figures who, from our vantage point on the world, appear to possess personal traits and/or perform actions that exemplify our conception of our ideal self, the self that our personal or group history, in the best of all possible worlds, has prepared us to become.[37]

Slaves in the Americas needed to survive a system that deprived them of liberty and the most basic human needs such as food and clothing. Thus, among other heroic figures, these slaves retrieved from their African heritage the wily trickster. Since Jim Crow laws not only denied them the protection of law, but served as an instrument for their continued oppression, the outlaw who could beat the law became their hero/heroines. According to Roberts, figures and actions considered heroic in one historical context or by one group of people may be viewed as ordinary or even criminal in another historical context, by other groups, or even by the same groups at different times. Yet, they become heroic—endowed with charisma—when through the telling and retelling of their stories they serve a given people's need for heroes and heroines to help them meet the challenges they face. It is this process that prophetic Christian education seeks to replicate as it tells the story of an ordinary carpenter, executed as a common criminal, but endowed with heroic charisma for all time.

Thee Smith has observed in *Conjuring Culture*,[38] Jesus Christ has been such a metaphorical hero/heroine for centuries in the Western World and a significant portion of humankind,

> because of his multiple persona as (1) cosmic lord and divine logos—the word of God by whom all things were created and subsist; (2) an earthly

(Davidic) king, heir of an ancient dynasty and of a messianic destiny of imperial power and rule; and (3) a religious leader of miraculous and prophetic powers who represents and mediates divine favor and judgment, beneficence and justice, to the acclaim and prosperity of his people and all Nations.[39]

Today's religious education fails, however, to provide adequate metaphors of Jesus capable of attracting significant charisma and dignity among African Americans to become a heroic model and liberating force. Hence the first task of a prophetic Christian religious education is to tell stories that promote the historicity, relevance, and seriousness of Jesus' metaphorical persona and transhistorical nature. The persona of metaphor for Jesus Christ is endowed with charisma when his metaphors have historicity, relevance, and seriousness, when (1) we recognize in Jesus the transhistorical possibilities in one person to challenge historical structures of oppression and achieve transhistorical salvation; (2) we see the significant role Jesus plays for us in the ongoing drama of liberation, reconciliation, and transformation; and (3) we let Jesus become for us the ultimate model of dignity and heroic action. From this perspective, a prophetic Christian education then becomes a system of charismatic legitimization of Christ for today.[40]

Anne S. Wimberly in *Soul Stories: African American Christian Education* uses such a heroic, story-driven metaphorical process in her work.

> Story-linking is a process whereby we connect parts of our everyday stories with the Christian faith story in the Bible and the lives of exemplars of the Christian faith outside the Bible. In this process, we link with Bible stories by using them as mirrors through which we reflect critically on the liberation we have already found or are still seeking. We also link with our Christian faith heritage by learning about exemplars who chose a way of living based on their understanding of liberation and vocation found in Scripture. By linking with Christian faith heritage stories, we may be encouraged and inspired by predecessors who have faced life circumstances with which we readily identify.[41]

Story-linking is a metaphorical process that focuses on the heroic to provide a transcendent self-identity. As an educational process, it overcomes the influence of double consciousness in the development of the social self by taking seriously the conditions of the material self by leading learners toward a third sense of self that transcends both material and social selves. This transcendent sense of self is a "spiritual self" based on mirror images found in a biblical perspective and heroic imagination.

Joseph Crockett and Anne Wimberly were both influenced by the person and work of Grant Shockley, especially in the emphasis they place on liberation and transformation. They each engage the metaphorical task of a prophetic Christian education in their quest for sources in the biblical and cultural traditions of African Americans for metaphors to carry God's vision for the contemporary and future black church.

Prophesying into Our Historical Context

At the beginning of the twentieth century, DuBois proclaimed that the problem of the coming century would be the "color line." At the advent of the twenty-first century the "color line" is still a problem. The "poverty line," however, may well be the catalyst to an even greater crisis on a global scale. The line that separates the oppressed and the oppressor will increasingly not be the color of one's skin but the "color of money." The notion of oppressed and oppressor will become increasingly less personal and less localized, and increasingly more digital and more global. Christianity even within the United States may soon become a minority religion as whites become just another minority. How then will prophetic Christian education speak to what Paulo Freire would have called this new historical epoch?[42]

To answer this question we must ask four very practical questions. These questions in turn establish the framework for the development of specific Christian education strategies in congregations, in denominations, and across ecumenical and even inter-religious associations.

In a prophetic Christian education, what must be taught and learned? The stories of God's actions in history establish the framework for what must be taught and learned. The actions of God on behalf of oppressed peoples are retold in light of today's headlines and through the stories from the lives of contemporary people. Careful attention is paid to the metaphors in Scripture, such as the names for God, Jesus, and the people of God. Further attention to metaphorical depictions of historical epochs, God's actions, and the people's aspirations become windows into contemporary experience. Stories of the heroism of ordinary people from the Scriptures become contemporary examples. The central role of prophecies, visions, and prophets in the Old and New Testaments are carefully examined for ways they illumine and inform our lives today.

In a prophetic Christian education, teachers and learners also practice reading their own environments with a prophetic eye. This means, in the first place, developing competencies in practices of critical reflection and social analysis appropriate to the ages of learners as the means to creating knowledge rather than consuming information. This means in the second place that in a prophetic Christian education teachers and students reflectively act on the knowledge they have created in ways congruent with their metaphorical understandings of God's nature, who they are, and the times in which they live.

In a prophetic Christian education, who teaches and who learns? And what is the role of pastors? In a sense everyone teaches and learns in a prophetic Christian education. Pastors, volunteer teachers, but perhaps, even more to the point, anyone who discerns a prophetic "word" for a given situation or setting may "teach." Prophetic teachers facilitate a cooperative, participatory, and charismatic process/event in which their teaching is distinguished, in part, by their own openness to learning. In a deeper sense, the Holy Spirit teaches as teachers and learners attend to the interplay of God's revealed Word in scripture and action in the world around them. From this perspective the pastor is a prophetic teacher/learner in a prophetic community. The prophetic teaching of pastors occurs not only in formal educational settings, but in worship events, through pastoral and administrative responsibilities, and in the public roles of community leadership. Pastoral prophetic teaching, like any prophetic teaching, grows out of and relies upon a prophetic imagination and vocation.

In a prophetic Christian education, what does teaching and learning look like? At one level teaching is a process of facilitation, modeling, and prophetic guidance. In this sense, prophetic Christian education gathers learners into a participatory educational process. Teachers and learners develop the capacity to share their gifts of the Spirit with others. They cooperate in the adventure of discovering God's word, reading the world, and producing new knowledge of their environment. They engage in a metaphorical praxis aimed at the transformation of oppressive conditions according to God's Word as they discern it through critical reflection. This metaphorical praxis involves three interdependent movements for teachers and students: (1) the telling and retelling of the stories of God's activity in the Scriptures; (2) linking those ancient stories to contemporary stories in a praxis of transformative imagination; and (3) discerning or "seeing the world" in which they live through the stories of God's activity recorded in the scripture to the end that they are renewed and energized for prophetic living through their growing awareness of God's presence in the course of contemporary events.

In a prophetic Christian education, where does teaching and learning occur? Teaching and learning occur wherever the people of God are gathered or scattered. By its very nature a prophetic Christian education must engage the community wherever Christians find themselves. A prophetic Christian education may occur in classroom settings but is never limited to the classroom. It may occur in church buildings but is never limited to the church building. Teaching and learning may take place on a picket line, as it did for many during the Civil Rights Movement, as well as in a Bible study group; in the legislature as well as in services of worship; in corporate boardrooms as well as in Sunday schools. As a praxis education, teaching and learning takes place in the midst of the action and reflection of the people of God engaged in the transformation of their communities and world according to the Spirit and Word of God.

Grant Shockley devoted his life to the task of discerning the sources of Christian education in the experience of African American Christians. He traced that experience back through the story of the African American presence in the Americas. The developments in Black Theology and liberative pedagogy provided sources for new and constructive approaches to Christian education—an education that emphasized the liberative and prophetic dimensions of the gospel in the heritage of African Americans. He laid the groundwork for the approach to prophetic Christian education that we have outlined above as he has for the work of Anne Wimberly, Joseph Crockett, and other African American Christian education scholars, some of whom are just beginning to contribute to the larger conversation on Christian education out of the black religious experience. He was truly prophetic, a trailblazer of freedom through the bondage of double consciousness, in the quest for a religious education that could be truly liberative for all. In our own quest for a prophetic Christian education, we have relied on his vision. We have been sustained by his persistence. And we have been inspired by his courage. He was for us, a prophetic Christian educator.

Appendix

Grant S. Shockley's Curriculum Vita

Education

A.B. degree, 1942, Lincoln University, Lincoln University, PA
M.Div. degree, 1945, Drew University, Madison, NJ
M.A. degree, 1946, Columbia University, New York, NY
Ed.D. degree, 1952, Columbia University/Union Theological Seminary, New York, NY

Professional Experience

Ministerial

Assistant Minister, St. Mark's United Methodist Church, New York, NY, 1942–46

Minister, Whatcoat Memorial United Methodist Church Dover, DE, 1951–53

Minister, Janes Memorial United Methodist Church Brooklyn, NY, 1953–59

Teaching

Instructor, Bible, Religion, and Philosophy, Clark College, Atlanta, GA, 1946–49

Professor, Religious Education, Gammon Theological Seminary
Atlanta, GA, 1949–51

Lecturer, Religious Education, New York University,
New York, NY, 1957–59

Professor, Religious Education, Garrett Theological Seminary
Evanston, IL, 1959–66

Lecturer, Religion, College of Liberal Arts, Northwestern University
Evanston, IL, 1960–63

Professor of Christian Education, Candler School of Theology, Emory
    University
Atlanta, GA, 1970–75

Lecturer, Religion, College of Liberal Arts, Emory University
Atlanta, GA, 1970–75

Professor, Christian Education, The Divinity School, Duke University
Durham, NC, 1983–89

Visiting Professorships

Centro Evangelico Unido, Mexico, D.F., Fall, 1966
Union Theological Seminary, New York, NY, Summer, 1967
Drew Theological Seminary, Madison, NJ, Spring, 1968
Perkins School of Theology, Southern Methodist University, Dallas,
    TX, Summer, 1970
Iliff School of Theology, Denver, CO, Summer, 1971
University of Zimbabwe, Harare, Zimbabwe, Summer, 1985
Candler School of Theology, Emory University, 1989–91
Clark Atlanta University, 1991–95

Administration

Executive Secretary, Interboard Committee on Christian Education,
    World Division, Board of Global Ministries, The United Methodist

Church, New York, NY (educational consultation in countries in Africa, Asia, Europe, Latin America and North America) 1966–70

President, The Interdenominational Theological Center, Atlanta, GA 1975–79

President, Philander Smith College, Little Rock, AR, 1979–83

NOTES

Foreword

1. W. E. B. DuBois, *The Souls of Black Folk* (New York: Bantam Books, 1989): 3.

2. Other prominent African American religious educators giving significant leadership in the field included: Olivia Pearl Stokes, James D. Tyms, Paul Nichols, Mary Love, Yvonne Delk, and Willard A. Williams.

Section I. A Way of Thinking About the Black Religious Experience

1. B. L. Putnam Weale. *The Conflict of Color* (New York: Macmillan, 1910): 228.

2. W. E. B. DuBois. *The Souls of Black Folk* (Chicago: A.C. McClurg & Co., 1903): 3.

3. Winthrop D. Jordan. *White over Black: American Attitudes Toward the Negro 1550–1812* (Baltimore: Penguin, 1968): 20.

4. Henry A. Bullock, *A History of Negro Education in the South from 1619 to the Present* (Cambridge: Harvard University Press, 1967): 11-12.

5. Lerone Bennett, Jr., *Before the Mayflower, A History of the Negro in America 1619–1964* (Baltimore: Penguin Books, 1966: 30; W. E. B. DuBois, *The Negro Church* (Atlanta: The Atlanta University Press, 1903): section 8, 110.

6. Margaret A. Diggs, *Catholic Negro Education in the United States* (n.p. 1936): 2-3.

7. DuBois, *The Negro Church*, 8.

8. Charles C. Jones, *The Religious Instruction of Negroes in the United States* (Savannah: Thomas Purse, 1842): 8.

9. George Stewart, Jr., A *History of Religious Education in Connecticut to the Middle of the Nineteenth Century* (New Haven: Yale University Press, 1924): 182.

10. W. D. Weatherford, *American Churches and the Negro* (Boston: The Christopher Publishing House, 1957): 56.

11. Jones, *Religious Instruction*: 35-9, passim.

12. Harry E. Stocker, *A Home Mission History of the Moravian Church in the United States and Canada* (The Special Publication Committee of the Moravian Church, 1924): 14, 15, 29, 38, 61, 240-41; Jones, *Religious Instuction*: 30-31, 57, 64-65, 66-67, 69.

13. Addie G. Wardle, *History of the Sunday School Movement in the Methodist Episcopal Church* (New York: Methodist Book Concern, 1918): 45-49, 52-65; Jones, *Religious Instruction*: 54-55.

14. Carter G. Woodson, *The Education of the Negro Prior to 1861* (New York: G. P. Putnam, 1915): 112-13.

15. DuBois, *The Negro Church*; 22.

16. Woodson, *The Education of the Negro*, 114.

17. Woodson, *The Education of the Negro*, 124.

18. Lawrence N. Jones, "They Sought a City: The Black Church and the Churchmen in the Nineteenth Century," *Union Seminary Quarterly Review*, Vol. XXVI, No. 3, Spring, 1971: 267.

19. William E. Capers, *Catechism: For the Use of Methodist Mission*, Part First (Nashville: Southern Methodist Publishing House, 1857. Revised in 1880 by T. O. Summers).

20. William N. Hartshorn, ed. *An Era of Progress and Promise, 1863–1910* (Boston: Pricilla Pub. Co., 1910): 11-27.

21. Daniel A. Payne, *History of the African Methodist Episcopal Church* (Nashville: A.M.E. Sunday School Union, 1891).

22. Compare Grant S. Shockley, "The A.M.E. and The A.M.E. Zion Churches," *The History of American Methodism* (Vol. II): 569-72.

23. James D. Tyms, *The Rise of Religious Education Among Negro Baptists* (New York: Exposition Press, 1965).

Section II. Sources for a Liberative Religious Education

1. Compare Van A. Harvey, *A Handbook of Theological Terms* (New York: Macmillan, 1964): 242-43.

2. Michael B. Foster, *Mystery and Philosophy* (London: SCM Press, 1957):18-19.

3. J. D. B. Miller, *The Politics of the Third World* (London: Oxford University Press, 1966): xi.

4. Ibid.

5. Vera Micheles Dean, *The Nature of Non-Western World* (New York: New American Library, 1963): 14.

6. Ibid., 15.

7. Ibid., 14.

8. Richard Hensman, *From Gandhi to Guevara: The Polemics of Revolt* (London: Allen Lane, The Penguin Press, 1970): 72.

9. Paul E. Johnson, *The Psychology of Religion* (New York: Abingdon, 1959): 53.

10. Peter L. Berger, *A Rumor of Angels* (Garden City, N.Y.: Doubleday, 1970): 3.

11. Mircea Eliade, *The Sacred and the Profane* (New York: Harper, 1959): 188.

12. Vittorio Lanternari, *The Religions of the Oppressed* (New York: New American Library, 1963): vi-vii.

13. Bishop S. Kulandran, *Resurgent Religions* (London: Lutterworth Press, 1957): 7.

14. Richard A. Long, "Negritude," *Negro Digest* (May 1969): 11.

15. Quoted in John S. Mbiti, *African Religions and Philosophy* (New York: Praeger, 1960): 267.

16. Ibid., 268.

17. Ibid.

18. Ibid.

19. Quoted in Colin Legun, *Pan-Africanism: A Short Political Guide* (New York: Praeger, 1965): 119.

20. Mbiti, *African Religions and Philosophy:* 271.

21. Herbert A. Richardson and Donald R. Cutler (eds.), *Transcendence* (Boston: Beacon Press, 1969): 9.

22. Ibid., 56.

23. Ibid., 54.

24. J. DaViega Coutinho, "Your Church and the Third World," *New World Outlook* (February 1970): 22.

25. "Eternity here doesn't denote everlastingness—continuance in time forever—but rather total presence in the present: Eckhart's 'Now moment,' Buddha's 'single instant awakening,' Wittgenstein's 'He lives eternally who lives in the present.'" Compare Richardson, *Transcendence:* 4-5.

26. Lantenari, The Religions of the Oppressed: x.

27. Berger, A Rumor of Angels.

28. Richardson, *Transcendence*, 6.

29. Berger, *A Rumor of Angels*, 95-96.

30. W. E. B. DuBois, *The Souls of Black Folk* (Chicago: A. C. McClurg and Co., 1903): 13; Martin Weinberg, ed., *W.E.B. DuBois: Reader* (New York: Harper & Row, 1970): 15.

31. Lerone Bennett, *The Challenge of Education*, Black Paper no. 1 (Atlanta: Institute of the Black World, April, 1970); Paulo Freire, "Witness of Liberation," *Seeing Education Whole* (Geneva: World Council of Churches, 1970), 72.

32. Rosemary R. Ruether, "Education in the Sociological Situation, U.S.A. (Part A)," in Kendig B. Cully, ed., *Does the Church Know How to Teach? An*

Ecumenical Inquiry (New York: The Macmillan Co., 1970): 79; see Arnold S. Nash, *Protestant Thought in the Twentieth Century: When and Whither* (New York: The Macmillan Co., 1951); John Dillenberger and Claude Welch, Protestant Christianity (New York: Charles Scribner's Sons, 1954).

33. Compare Reinhold Niebuhr, *Moral Man and Immoral Society* (New York: Charles Scribner's Sons, 1932): 119, 208, 251-55, 268, 272.

34. See George Albert Coe, *What Is Religion Doing to Our Consciences?* (New York: Charles Scribner's Sons, 1943): 8, especially, 31, 48, 78, 82-83, 91-92, 98-99; Compare Robert W. Lynn and Elliott Wright, *The Big Little School: Sunday Child of American Protestantism* (New York: Harper & Row, 1971), chap. 2.

35. Quoted from Louis Weeks, "Horace Bushnell on Black America," *Religious Education*, 68 (January-April, 1973), 28-41.

36. Randolph Crump Miller, "From Where I Sit: Some Issues in Christian Education," *Religious Education* 60 (March-April, 1965), 102-3.

37. The title of the book, *The Wretched of the Earth*, by the black North African intellectual and revolutionist Frantz Fanon.

38. Editor's note: The Curriculum Resources Committee and the Board of Discipleship are agencies responsible for the oversight of educational ministries in The United Methodist Church.

39. "Black Power: Statement by National Committee of Negro Churcmen," *New York Times*, 31 (July 1966): E-5f.

40. Ibid.

41. *The Uppsala 68 Report* (Geneva: World Council of Churches, 1968): 241.

42. Dee Brown, *Bury My Heart at Wounded Knee* (New York: Holt, Rinehart and Winston, 1971): chaps. 1-2.

43. *The Works of John Wesley*, vol. 13 (Grand Rapids, Mich.: Zondervan, n.d.): 153).

44. Milton L. Barron, ed., *Minorities in a Changing World* (New York: Knopf, 1967): chaps. 3-4; George E. Simpson and J. Milton Yinger, *Racial And Cultural Minorities* (New York: Harper & Brothers, 1953): chaps. 11-15; Philip Hayasaka, "The Asian Experience in White America," *Journal of Intergroup Relations*, 2 (Spring 1973): 67-73.

45. James H. Cone, "Black Consciousness and the Black Church: A Historical-Theological Interpretation," *Annals of the American Academy of Political and Social Science* 387 (January 1970): 33.

46. Joseph R. Washington, *Black Religion* (Boston: Beacon Press, 1964).

47. See *Black Theology: A Critical Assessment*, comp. James H. Evans, Jr. (New York: Greenwood Press, 1987) for an excellent coverage of the literature of black theology.

48. See James H. Cone and Gayraud S. Wilmore, eds., *Black Theology: A Documentary History, 1966–1979*, Vol. 1 (Maryknoll, N.Y.: Orbis, 1993), especially Part VI: 349-454.

49. See ibid. Part V, 279-348 for the best available coverage of black theology and women's issues.

50. James H. Cone, *Black Theology and Black Power* (New York: Seabury, 1969). Also see Cone's *A Black Theology of Liberation* (Philadelphia: Westminster, 1970).

51. See Cecil W. Cone, *Identity Crisis in Black Theology* (Nashville: African Methodist Episcopal Church, 1975).

52. Leon E. Wright, "Black Theology or Black Experience?" *Journal of Religious Thought* (Summer 1969): 46.

Section III. The Quest for a Model

1. Leon E. Wright, " 'Black Theology' or Black Experience?" *Journal of Religious Thought* (Summer 1969): 46.

2. National Committee of Black Church Mission Statement (1966).

3. "Black Power," *Statement by National Committee of Negro Churchmen* (New York: Commission on Religion and Race, National Council of Churches, July 1966).

4. Frazier and Lincoln, pp. 105-6.

5. Gayraud S. Wilmore, "The Case for a New Black Church Style," in *The Black Experience in Religion*, ed. C. Eric Lincoln (New York: Anchor Press/Doubleday, 1974): 34-44.

6. C. D. Coleman, "Agenda for the Black Church," *Religious Education* (November-December, 1969): 441-46.

7. Paulo Freire, *Pedagogy of the Oppressed* (New York: Herder and Herder, 1971).

8. A cursory survey of the literature in the field of religious education from the Black perspective indicates relatively few books but numerous articles. *The Religious Instruction of the Negroes in the United States* by Charles C. Jones (Savannah: T. Purse, 1842) stands alone until the present century. In 1910, William N. Hartshorn in his edited volume, *An Era of Progress and Promise 1863-1910: The Clifton Conference*, describes the Clifton Plan for religious education to be offered among Blacks by Black college students and graduates (Boston: Pricille Publishing Co., 1910). *Religious Education* published its first essay on Blacks and religious education in 1912. This discussion of Negro Sunday schools was written by Wilbur P. Thirkeild and appeared in Vol. VII, April 1912. Carter G. Woodson also made several significant statements about the religious instruction of Blacks in his classic study, *The Education of the Negro Prior to 1861* (New York: G. O. Putnam, 1915).

The subject of religious education among Black people during the 1920s was generally neglected. In the 1930s a spate of writings appear. J. L. Carter wrote on "The Negro Vacation Church School," a first article of its kind for the recently new International Journal of Religious Education (Vol. 7:22, March, 1931). In 1936, Margaret A. Diggs wrote her Catholic Negro Education in the United States (n.p.). John Dillingham wrote Making Religious Education Effective (New York: Association Press, 1935). I. Mays and Joseph W. Nicholson reported a significant set of statistics about Black Sunday schools in The Negro's Church (1933). In 1936 Charles H. Wesley authored an important article in the Journal of Negro History (Vol. 21, October, 1936, pp. 376-93), entitled "The Religious Attitudes of Negro Youth." Educator G. Daniel wrote an article entitled "The Role of Youth Character Building Organizations in Juvenile Delinquent Prevention" in the Journal of Negro Education (Vol. 28, Summer, 1959), pp. 310-17.

In 1964 as a part of a chapter history of the AME and AME Zion Churches in Emory S. Bucke's *History of American Methodism* (Vol. 2), the writer traced Christian education in the life of these two Black Methodist denominations (pp. 526-82). James D. Tyms published in 1965, his Boston University doctoral dissertation, *The Rise of Religious Education Among Negro Baptists: A Historical Case Study.* In 1968 Joseph W. Nicholson reported some further data on Sunday school enrollment and attendance in Black churches of the Protestant Episcopal Church in *What Is Happening to the Negro in the Protestant Episcopal Church* (privately published). Four important articles appeared in the 1969 convention issue of *Religious Education* (Vol. XIV, No. 6 [Nov.-Dec.]): Thomas E. Brown, "Sex Education and Life in the Black Ghetto"; C. D. Coleman, "Agenda for the Black Church"; Joseph A. Johnson, "The Imperative of Beyondness"; and Andrew White, "Why the Church Should Evangelize Black Youth."

The 1970s has been the most productive decade thus far in the publication of resources on the religious education of Blacks. *Spectrum: International Journal of Religious Education* (Vol. 47, No. 4, July-August, 1971), devoted a special issue to the subject. Articles included "Education of Blacks in the Household of Faith" by Olivia P. Stokes, pp. 5-7; "Saturday Ethnic School: A Model" by John H. Adams (pp. 8-10); "The Role of the Black Church in the Liberation Struggles" by Andrew White (pp. 10-12); "Three R's in Theology" by George Thomas (p. 13); "The Relational Imperative" by James E. Massey (pp. 13-15); and "Social Contexts for Black Christian Education" by Robert O. Dulin, Jr. (pp. 19-21). In 1972, Olivia Pearl Stokes wrote a provocative article, "Blacks, Engagement, and Action" (*Religious Education*, Vol. LXXII, 1972 [January-February], pp. 22-24. During 1973, Riggins R. Earl, Jr. edited *To You Who Teach in the Black Church* (Nashville: The National Baptist Publishing Board). Also in 1973 the United Church of Christ Press issued its useful packet, *New Roads to Faith: Black Perspectives in Church Education* including the "Acts of God" by Vincent Harding: "Educating Black People for Liberation and Collective Growth" by James M. Jones; and "The Educational Role of Black Churches in the 70's and 80's" by Olivia Pearl Stokes. In 1974 a symposium, "Educating in the Black Church" appeared in *Religious Education* (Vol. LXIX, No. 4, [July-

August], 1974), and Willard A. Williams edited *Educational Ministries with Blacks* (Nashville: Board of Discipleship, 1974). Two publications of note appeared in 1978: Bennie E. Goodwin's *Reflections on Education*, Atlanta: Goodpatrick Publishers, and Thomas L. Webber's *Deep Like the Rivers: Education in the Slave Quarter Community, 1831–1865* (New York: W. W. Morton).

Several works have also been published since 1980. In 1982 Janice E. Hale published *Black Children: Their Roots, Culture, and Learning Styles* (Provo: Brigham Young University Press). That same year Nathan Jones published *Sharing the Old, Old Story: Educational Ministry in the Black Community* (Winona, Minn.: St. Mary's Press). In 1984 Paul Nichols's essay "Blacks and the Religious Education Movement" was included in Marvin Taylor, ed. *Changing Patterns of Religious Education* (Nashville: Abingdon). Recently three publications of note have come from the press: *Teaching Strategies for Ethnic Studies* by James A. Banks (Boston: Allyn and Bacon, 1984); *Christian Education Journey of Black Americans: Past, Present, Future* (Nashville: Discipleship Resources, 1985); and Ella Mitchell, "Oral Tradition: Legacy of Faith for the Black Church," which appeared in *Religious Education* (Vol. 8, No. 1 [Winter], 1986).

9. Lawrence N. Jones, "They Sought a City: The Black Church and Churchmen in the Nineteenth Century," *Union Seminary Quarterly Review* (Vol. XXVI, No. 3 [Spring 1969]): 267.

10. Leon E. Wright, "Black Theology or Black Experience?" *Journal of Religious Thought* (Summer 1969): 46.

11. "Black Power: Statement by the National Committee of Negro Churchmen." Cited in *Black Theology: A Documentary History, 1966–1979*, ed. Gayraud S. Wilmore and James N. Cone (New York: Orbis Books, 1979): 23-30.

12. W. E. B. DuBois, *The Souls of Black Folk* (Chicago: A. C. McClurg Co., 1903).

13. Winthrop D. Jordan, *White Over Black: American Attitudes Toward the Negro, 1550–1812* (Baltimore: Penguin, 1968): 20.

14. Paul F. Knitter, *No Other Name: A Critical Survey of Christian Attitudes Toward the World Religions* (Maryknoll, N.Y.: Orbis, 1985): 207.

15. Ibid., 207-11.

16. Ibid., 209.

17. W. E. B. DuBois, *The Souls of Black Folk* (Chicago: A. C. McClurg, 1903): 3.

18. James A. Geschwender, *Racial Stratification in America* (Dubuque, Iowa: W. C. Brown, 1978): 55.

19. Jordan, 20.

20. Frank S. Loescher, *The Protestant Church and the Negro: A Pattern of Segregation* (New York: Association Press, 1948): 27.

21. *"Black Power": Statement by National Committee of Negro Churchmen* (New York: Commission on Religion and Race, National Council of Churches, 1966).

22. Gayraud S. Wilmore and James H. Cone, *Black Theology: A Documentary History, 1966–1979* (Maryknoll, N.Y.: Orbis, 1979): 445-60.

23. John B. Cobb, "The Meaning of Pluralism for Christian Self-Understanding," in Leroy S. Rouner, ed., *Religious Pluralism* (Notre Dame: University of Notre Dame Press, 1984): 173.

24. Walter Watson, *The Architectonics of Meaning: Foundations of New-Pluralism* (Albany: State University Press of New York, 1955): ix.

25. Gayraud S. Wilmore, "The Case for a New Black Church Style," in *The Black Experience in Religion*, ed. C. Eric Lincoln (Garden City, N.Y.: Doubleday, 1974): 34-44.

26. This sixth point was not developed in the essay. (Eds.)

27. James H. Cone, "Black Consciousness and the Black Church: A Historical-Theological Interpretation," *Annals of the American Academy of Political and Social Science* (January 1970): 53.

28. William R. Jones, "Assessment of Black Theology" (n.p.).

29. Herbert Richardson as quoted in *Roots of Resistance: The Nonviolent Ethic of Martin Luther King, Jr.* (Valley Forge: Judson, 1985): 15.

30. Donald E. Miller, "Religious Education and Social Change" (an unpublished paper presented at the Professors and Researchers in Religious Education, February, 8-9, 1969): p. 1; also see his *Story and Context: An Introduction to Christian Education* (Nashville: Abingdon, 1987).

31. Bennie E. Goodwin, *Reflections on Education: A Christian Scholar Looks at King, Freire, and Jesus* (Atlanta: Goodpatrick, 1978): chap. 2.

32. Peter L. Berger, *The Noise of Solemn Assemblies* (Garden City, N.Y.: Doubleday, 1961): 116.

33. Miller, "Religious Education and Social Change," 3.

34. Dieter T. Hessel, "A Whole Ministry of (Social) Education," *Religious Education* 78:4 (Fall 1983), 525-59.

35. Gayraud S. Wilmore, "The Case for a New Black Church Style," in *The Black Experience and Religion*, ed., C. Eric Lincoln (Garden City, NY: 1974): 33-44.

36. Ian G. Barbour, *Myths, Models and Paradigms; A Study in Science and Religion* (New York: Harper & Row, 1974): 8.

37. K. B. Cully and F. Niles Harper, *Will the Church Lose the City?* (New York: World, 1969).

38. Robert McAfee Brown, "Doing Theology Today: Some Footnotes on Theological Method," *Action-Reflection* (Summer 1969): 3-4.

39. Paulo Freire, *Pedagogy of the Oppressed* (New York: Herder and Herder, 1970): 33-34.

40. Susan Thistlethwaite, "Peace and Justice, Not issues but Identities for the Church," *Engage/Social Action* (January 1987): 33.

41. Dieter T. Hessel, *Social Ministry* (Philadelphia: Westminster, 1982): 198.

42. Sara Little, *To Set One's Heart: Belief and Teaching in the Church* (Atlanta: John Knox, 1983): 76-79.

43. James B. McGinnis, "Educating for Peace and Justice," *Religious Education* (Summer 1986): 446-65.

44. See Suzanne Toten, "Structural Change: The Next Step in Justice Education," *Religious Education* (Summer 1985).

45. Peter Berger, *The Precarious Vision* (New York: Doubleday, 1961): 111.

46. The pioneering work of Yvonne Delk is related by Delores H. Carpenter in an article, "Interpreting the History of Religious Education in the Twentieth Century," *Religious Education* 88:4 (Fall 1993): 622-23.

47. For additional information see Olivia P. Stokes, "Black Theology: A Challenge to Religious Education," in *Religious Education and Theology*, ed. Norma H. Thompson (Birmingham: Religious Education Press, 1982).

48. Ella P. Mitchell discusses her contextual mode in some detail in her article "Oral Tradition: Legacy of Faith for the Black Church," *Religious Education* 81:1 (Winter 1986): 93-112.

49. In his *Teaching Scripture from an African-American Perspective* (Nashville: Discipleship Resources, 1990), Joseph V. Crockett gives careful attention to the use of the Bible in the black educational experience.

50. See William Julius Wilson, *The Truly Disadvantaged* (Chicago: University of Chicago Press, 1987).

51. See Walter Brueggemann, *Living Toward a Vision* (New York: United Church Press, 1982): 15.

52. Paul L. Lehmann, "The Shape of Theology for a World in Revolution," *Motive* (April 1965): 9.

53. Dieter T. Hessel, *Social Ministry* (Philadelphia: Westminster, 1982): 18.

54. George E. Koehler, "Some Methodist Hopes for a New Educational Ministry," *Religious Education* (May-June, 1966).

55. Randolph Crump Miller, "From Where I Sit: Some Issues in Christian Education," *Religious Education* (March-April 1965): 101.

56. Freire, *Pedagogy of the Oppressed*, 75.

57. William R. Jones, "Toward an Interim Assessment of Black Theology," *Christian Century* 89, 3 (May 1972): 513-17.

58. Herbert Richardson, as quoted in William D. Wately, *Roots of Resistance: The Non-Violent Ethic of Martin Luther King, Jr.* (Valley Forge, Pa.: Judson, 1985): 15.

Section IV. To Create the Beloved Community

1. Shockley, "Does the Church Really Want Religious Education," p. 221.

2. Shockley, "From Emancipation to Transformation to Consummation," p. 221.

3. Shockley, "Black Pastoral Leadership in Religious Education . . . ," pp. 179-80.

4. Ibid., p. 182.

5. Theodore E. Long, "Prophecy, Charisma, and Politics: Reinterpreting the Weberian Thesis," Jeffrey K. Hadden and Anson Shupe, eds., Prophetic Religions and Politics: Religion and the Political Order, I (New York: Paragon House, 1986).

6. Max Weber's historical and theoretical work on prophecy includes The Theory of Social and Economic Organization (1947), Ancient Judaism (1952), Sociology of Religion (1963), and Economy and Society Theory (1978). In these works Weber conceives prophets as persons with exceptional powers who claim leadership on the basis of charismatic authority recognized by a group of followers as exemplary (1947, p. 359). The Prophet's exceptional quality opposes rational and traditional authority, exists as a revolutionary force, and establishes new obligations (1947, p. 361).

7. Long, "Prophecy, Charisma, and Politics," p. 4.

8. Ibid.

9. Long, "A Theory of Prophetic Religion and Politics," in Jeffrey K. Hadden and Anson Shupe, eds., Religion and the Political Order II (New York: Paragon House, 1988): 5.

10. These characteristics were adapted from Trevor Ling's discussion in Prophetic Religion (New York: Macmillan, 1966): 56.

11. Shockley, "Christian Education and the Black Religious Experience," p. 38.

12. William James, The Varieties of Religious Experience: A Study in Human Nature (New York: Longmans, Green & Co., 1902).

13. Cornel West, Prophecy/Deliverance: An Afro-American Revolutionary Christianity (Philadelphia: Westminster Press, 1982): 16-20.

14. Ibid., p. 16.

15. Desmond Mpilo Tutu, No Future Without Forgiveness (New York: Random House, 1999): 31.

16. Warren R. Wise, "America's Most Critical Need: A Renaissance of Personal Moral Values," The Aspen Institute Quarterly, Vol. 5, No. 4 (Autumn 1993): 118.

17. Compare Josiah Royce, The Philosophy of Loyalty (New York: The Macmillan Company, 1920), 318, 403-4.

18. Romney Moseley, "Conversion: Healthy Religion and Public Life," unpublished, 2.

19. Don Browning, Pluralism and Personality (London: Associated University Presses, 1980): 90.

20. Ibid.

21. James, 1890, 1950, I: 297.

22. DuBois, p. 215.

23. Ibid.

24. Wade Boykin, "The Triple Quandary and the Schooling of Afro-Americans," in Ulric Neisser, ed. *The School Achievement of Minority Children: New Perspectives* (Hillsdale, N.J.: Lawrence Erlbaum Associates, 1986): 66.

25. Ibid., 66, 67.

26. Erik Erikson, *Identity, Youth and Crisis* (New York: W. W. Norton & Co., 1968): 303.

27. Shockley, "Christian Education and the Black Religious Experience," p. 39.

28. West's discussion of prophetic Christianity may be found in *Prophecy/Deliverance: An Afro-American Revolutionary Christianity.*

29. I will expand on my understanding of heroic below.

30. West, pp. 19-20.

31. Tutu's theological model seeks to restore the oppressor's humanity by releasing and enabling the oppressed to see their oppressors as peers under God. This can develop into a mutual understanding, as Jesus teaches, through friendship (John 15:15). For Tutu, *ubuntu* expresses this mutuality. The relationship of oppressor and oppressed and the resulting definition of humanity through racial classification are broken through *ubuntu*, an alternative way of being in a hostile world. See Michael Battle, *Reconciliation: The Ubuntu Theology of Desmond Tutu* (Cleveland: The Pilgrim Press, 1997): 5.

32. Trevor Ling, *Prophetic Religion* (New York: Macmillan and St. Martin's Press, 1966): 45-46.

33. Stanley Hauerwas, *Vision and Virtue: Essays in Christian Ethical Reflection* (Notre Dame: University of Notre Dame: 1981): 30.

34. Joseph V. Crockett, *Teaching Scripture: From an African-American Perspective* (Nashville: Discipleship Resources, 1990): 1-2.

35. Zora Neale Hurston, "Sometimes in the Mind," in Langston Hughes and Arna Bontemps, eds. *The Book of Negro Folklore* (New York: Dodd, Mead, 1958): 93; quoted in Riggins R. Earl, Jr., *Dark Symbols, Obscure Signs: God, Self, and Community in the Slave Mind* (Maryknoll, N.Y.: Orbis Books, 1993): 133.

36. Robert Penn Warren, "Introduction," in Dixon Wecter, *The Hero in America* (New York: Charles Scribner's Sons, 1972): xiv.

37. John W. Roberts, *From Trickster to Badman: The Black Folk Hero in Slavery and Freedom* (Philadelphia: University of Pennsylvania Press, 1989): 1.

38. Theophus Smith, *Conjuring Culture: Biblical Formations of Black America* (New York: Oxford University Press, 1994).

39. Ibid., p. 199.

40. Compare Anthony J. Blasi, *Making Charisma: The Social Construction of Paul's Public Image* (New Brunswick: Transaction Publishers, 1991): 11-12.

41. Anne Streaty Wimberly, *Soul Stories: African American Christian Education* (Nashville: Abingdon Press, 1994): 39.

42. The notion of historical epochs was developed by Paulo Freire. They are characterized by a series of aspirations, concerns, and values in search of fulfill-

ment, ways of being and behaving. The concrete representations of many of these aspirations, concerns, and values, as well as the obstacles to their fulfillment constitute the themes of any given epoch, which in turn indicates the task to be carried out. An epoch is fulfilled to the degree that its primary themes are grasped and its tasks solved. It is superseded when its themes and tasks no longer correspond to newly emerging concerns, values, or aspirations. See Freire, *Education for Critical Consciousness* (London: Shedd and Ward, 1973): 5.

SELECTED BIBLIOGRAPHY

Books: Religious Education

Brewer, Earl D. C.; Shockley, Grant S.; and Townsend, Marie. *Black Pastors and Churches in United Methodism*. Atlanta: Center for Research in Social Change, Emory University, 1976.

Foster, Charles R.; Johnson, Ethel R.; and Shockley, Grant S. Christian Education *Journey of Black Americans: Past, Present, and Future*. Nashville: Discipleship Resources, 1985.

Foster, Charles R. and Shockley, Grant S., eds. *Working with Black Youth*. Nashville: Abingdon Press, 1989.

Shockley, Grant S. *The New Generation in Africa*. New York: Friendship Press, 1971.

Books and Articles: Methodist Black Church

"The A.M.E. and the A.M.E. Zion Church," A *History of American Methodism*, E. S. Bucke, ed. Nashville: Abingdon, 1964.

"Black Leaders in Early American Methodism," *Bicentennial Historical Papers*, Albea Godbold, ed. Lake Junaluska, N.C.: Association of Methodist Historical Societies, 1967.

Encyclopedia of World Methodism, N. B. Harmon, ed. Nashville: The United Methodist Publishing House, 1974.

"Methodism and the Black Experience in America: A Study in Paradox and Potential," *Harris Franklin Rall Lecture*, Evanston, Ill.: Garrett-Evangelical Theological Seminary, 1973. (unpublished)

"Methodist, Society and Black Evangelism in America: Retrospect and Prospect," *A.M.E. Zion Quarterly Review*, July 1974.

"Methodists/United Methodists," *Encyclopedia of Black America*, W. A. Low, ed. New York: McGraw-Hill, 1981.

"Wesleyan Methodist in America: A Black Perspective," *Radix*, 1986.

Essays and Articles for Academic and Professional Readers

Shockley, Grant. S., General Editor. *Heritage and Hope: The African American Presence in United Methodism*. Nashville: Abingdon Press, 1991.

Essays and Articles for Professional and Academic Audiences

"Black Liberation, Christian Education and Black Church Indicators," *The Duke Divinity School Review*, Spring, 1975, Vol. 40, No. 2.

"Black Pastoral Leadership in Religious Education: Social Justice Correlates," *The Pastor as Religious Educator*, Robert L. Browning, ed. Birmingham: Religious Education Press, 1989.

"Black Theology and Religious Education," *Theologies of Religious Education*, Randolph Crump Miller, ed., Birmingham: Religious Education Press, 1995.

"Christian Education and the Black Religious Experience," *Ethnicity in the Education of the Church*, Charles R. Foster, ed. Nashville: Scarritt Press, 1987.

"Commentary on Plant Closures Project," *Pedagogues for the Non-Poor*, Alice F. Evans, Robert A. Evans, and William B. Kennedy, eds. New York: Orbis, 1987.

"Education," *Faith Meets Life* (Book Six), John P. Gilbert, ed. Nashville: Graded Press, 1983.

"Ethnic Pluralism and Future Forms of Ministry in the Military," *Military Chaplains Review*, Winter, 1978.

"From Emancipation to Transformation to Consummation: A Black Perspective," *Does the Church Really Want Religious Education?* Marlene Mayr, ed. Birmingham: Religious Education Press, 1988.

Harper's Encyclopedia of Religious Education. New York: Harper & Row, 1990.

"Liberation, Theology, Black Theology, and Religious Education," *Foundations for Christian Education in an Era of Change*, M. J. Taylor, ed. Nashville: Abingdon, 1976.

"Living Out the Gospel in Seminary Life," *The Christian Century*, February 2-9, 1977.

"National Church Bodies and Interdenominational Theological Education," *Theological Education*, Spring, 1979.

"Order, Change, and the Future: Naming Theological Education," *The Journal of the Interdenominational Theological Center*, Fall 1976, Vol. IV, No. 1.

"Religious Pluralism and Religious Education: A Black Protestant Perspective," *Religious Pluralism and Religious Education*, Norma H. Thompson, ed. Birmingham: Religious Education Press, 1994.

"Transcendence and Mystery in the Third World." *Transcendence and Mystery.* Earl D. C. Brewer, ed. New York: IDOC/North America, 1975.

Westminster Dictionary of Christian Education, K. B. Cully, ed. Philadelphia: Westminster, 1963.

"Worship in Christian Education," *An Introduction to Christian Education.* M. J. Taylor, ed. Nashville: Abingdon, 1966.

Articles for Local Church Audiences

"Christian Education," *Together* IX (Feb. 1965) 9:14-18.

"Christian Education in Sierra Leone," *Methodist Women*, XXVIII (March 1968) 7:14-16.

"Christian Education in Urban East Asia," *Response*, I (April, 1969) 4:14-17.

"Christian Public Opinion," *Church School*, XVI (Dec. 1962) 3:12-13.

"The Church, Revolution, and World Community," *Church School* (II (Dec., 1969): 16-17.

"Letter Box," *Church School* (Sept. 1965–Feb. 1966).

"The Use of Focus," *Church School*, V (Nov. 1972) 3:16-24.

3rd world defined   p. 51
prophetic   C E   142

Printed in the United States
30325LVS00006B/121-138

9 780687 044795